World Care
in Uncertain Times

Deena Larsen

©2024 Deena Larsen

Wonderbox Publishing
Llanerchymedd, Wales
United Kingdom

All rights reserved. No part of this book may be reproduced or used in any manner without the prior written permissions of the copyright owner, except for the use of brief quotations in a book review.

Some sample scenarios in this book are fictitious. Any similarity to actual persons, living or dead, is coincidental.

The information in this book was correct at the time of publication, but the author does not assume any liability for loss or damage caused by errors or omissions.

To request permissions, contact the publisher at wonderboxpublishing@gmail.com.

This edition is designed for Kindle Direct Publishing to distribute on Amazon. It is part of a two-part series (Self Care and World Care in Uncertain Times).

First paperback edition November 2024.

Edited by Lyle Skains.

Explanatory graphics by Lissy Salgado and Clarie Leyden.

Cover art and journal graphics by Deena Larsen, Rebecca Hamilton, and Claire Leyden.

Colophon

Cover art was designed using prompts in MidJourney Versions 3, 4, and 5 and then corrected in Photoshop and other graphic programs.

Fonts used are Google Fonts with an Open Font License: Rosario, Tinos, and Waiting for the Sunrise.

When people in your community cannot agree on what is more or less likely to happen in the future, you are working within the realm of deep uncertainty. You need to develop robust plans that will work under a wide range of futures. This planning is termed *Decision-making under Deep Uncertainty*. This book explores the concepts used to address complex problems with unknown outcomes—and explains how to integrate these concepts into your life and your community.

"If we can raise people's ability to manage uncertainty; there could be tangible opportunities for us to find new and better solutions to complex problems."

> Dr. Richard Plenty and Terri Morrissey, 2020.
> *Uncertainty Rules? Making Uncertainty Work for You.*

Table of Contents

This top sidebar explains the concepts.

Using these concepts will help you and your community plan for whatever futures actually happen.

Preface
Be a superhero in your life. i
Use this book to plan your life. ii

Introduction
Why you are here. iii
Why I am here iv

Part 1. Where are we?

Ground and Center: Who are you journeying with? 3
Social and Eco Systems: How does your community work within the world?. 5
Recognizing Change: What are the changes in your world? 9
Accepting Change How will your community handle change?. 11
Growth/Decay Cycle: What stages of change are the people, systems, and institutions in your communities in? 13
Traps: Where and why are we stuck? 15

Part 2. How can we understand change?

Information: What information can we use about our world?. 19
Change Network: How does change create more changes in an interconnected world? 21
Wicked Problems: How can we address tangled, messy problems? . 23
Deep Uncertainty: How can we prepare for what we don't know? . . 25
Vulnerability and Risk: Where could communities break down?. . . . 27

Part 3. How do we track changes?

Indicators: How can we track warning signs in the world?. 31
Resilience: How well can our community recover?. 33
Coping Range: How can we expand what our community can handle?. 35
Tipping Points: When does our community fail and transform into something new?. 37
Regime Shifts: How can we manage the new systems?. 39

This bottom sidebar suggests actions to help use these concepts in your community.

Look at the bottom of each page for content in the spillover website page. Selfcareworldcare.wikidot.com/toc has the table of contents so you can track each page of this workbook to a corresponding page on the website.

Table of Contents

Part 4. How can we plan for many futures?
Action Moments: How can prepare for opportunities to act? 43
Systems Planning: How can we think about these interconnected communities and processes?. 45
Scenarios: What wide range of futures can we imagine? 47
Resources: What can our community use? 49
Constraints and Limits: What can't our community do? 51

This book is organized by parts, which bring related concept steps together. Each concept has a question for your community to answer.

Part 5. What do we want—no matter what the future holds?
Goals and Objectives: What are our community's visions and goals? 55
Robust Objectives: What does our community absolutely need— no matter what? 57
Aligned Objectives: Does everyone see the same vision? 59
Robust Measurements: How can we measure our impacts in the real world? 61

Part 6. What can we do?
No- and Low-Regret Options: What can we do right away? 63
Creative Options: How can everyone think outside the lines? 65
Flexible Options: What actions can we use for many purposes? 67
Standardized Back-up Options: How can we continue if something fails? 69

While this book presents concepts step-by-step in a process, in reality you will skip around to think about these ideas and come back to concepts as you plan.

Part 7. What are our strategies?
Screen for Robust Options: What options will work? 73
Evaluate Options: What workable options are the best fit? 75
Stress Test: How well does this plan work for various factors under many scenarios? 77
Timing and Scaling: How can we grow and expand these plans? . . . 79

Part 8. Put those strategies to work!
Consequences and Trade-offs: How can this work for everyone? . . . 83
Adaptive Pathways: How can we plan for what-ifs and what-nows?. 85
Implementation: Put community plans in motion! 87
Adaptive Feedback Loop: Keep on planning and adapting! 89

Concepts will be mentioned throughout this book, and not in order. So you can come back to the table of contents and read about that concept.

Afterwards. 91

References. 93

Preface

Focus on one of your communities to work through this book.

Use this book for you and your community

This guide can help you and your community recognize and measure changes, adapt to what is happening, and transform your life and our worlds to successfully navigate these dynamic times. First off, of course, is the question:

Who are your communities?

You live in an intertangled, complex web of communities. Some are based on who you are, like your family, your friends, your buddies who share your interests, or a world-wide network of people who share your hobbies, your state, your nation. Others are based on where you are, like your neighborhood, city, state, country, and world. Each of these communities has its own spirit and vibrant life—from getting together for a family dinner to ensuring your streets are safe and clean to grappling with national economic woes.

Where will planning for uncertainty help the most?

All of our communities are adventuring into uncertain futures that could take many different paths. Your communities face change and uncertainty every day from complex problems with many factors, many participants, many causes, and many solutions—wicked problems. Problems like climate change, where a drought can dry up a water supply or threaten food or power production or a flood can wipe out whole cities. Or problems like the pollutants and microplastics in all of our bodies, oceans, and lands. If you like to surf, what will happen to your favorite beach in extreme storms or higher sea levels? If you like to ski, what would happen if the winter snow storms came later in the season and ended earlier? How will your family or neighborhood cope with droughts or famines that can cause changing prices or availability of goods?

For this workbook, pick one community to focus on, where changes seem particularly threatening and where you can have a voice to help others in your community plan together to face these threats. This could be your church, struggling to come back together after a disaster or a plague. Or your company, managing with war or disruptive technology. Or your scuba diving club, worried about coral bleaching from warmer oceans.

Choose your community, and gather a planning team. Make sure your community has the commitment to plan to thrive no matter what the future brings.

This workbook can help you work with your community to plan and prepare for whatever future comes your way. Decision-making under deep uncertainty is a new field of study that helps planners, stakeholders, community members, and decision-makers understand how to plan when no one knows what will happen in the future. This paper guide explains these concepts so that you can explain them and use them in your community planning. The electronic resources at *Selfcareworldcare.wikidot.com* provide references, examples, and more to get an even more comprehensive view of these planning concepts.

*Selfcareworldcare.wikidot.com/**toc**: The web table of contents so you can get more information.*

Plan together for changing futures

Why pick up this hard copy book? Because the world is changing rapidly, and you and your community need to adapt. This book explains how to plan and work together to help your community thrive—no matter what happens.

This book explains the basic concepts for Decision-making under Deep Uncertainty planning—a complex field used to plan for robust solutions that can function under a wide range of potential futures. Needless to say, each of these concepts is a field of study unto itself—and each of those fields involves other fields, and pretty soon there is an overwhelming tangle of potential paths to follow. Wow, this can get pretty overwhelming fast. Don't worry—in this workbook, I bring each of these planning concepts down from the academic to the practical. You do not have to know everything to start using these concepts in your community.

This workbook provides a page for each concept to help you talk to others and plan together so that you and your communities can prepare for, manage, and recover from changes in the face of many uncertain futures. After each text page is an art page with prompts to spark ideas and write observations. Or just to draw and doodle to help think.

Just get started here. I would suggest going through the concepts in more or less the order I have them to help you and others in your community plan out actions to thrive in a range of futures. To sprint through the book, look at the boxes in the margin, which provide a TLDR (too long didn't read) for each concept

You can go through the concepts that appeal to you in a bit more depth on each page, and then think about the prompting questions to integrate these concepts into your life. You can work with your community to help answer these questions as well.

But there is so much else out there! To head off the information overload, I have a "spillover electronic version" (http://selfcareworldcare.wikidot.com/) a dedicated wiki where you can step off into more and more:

- **Concepts and references.** I'll briefly explain concepts noted in the "More to explore" arrows on the bottom of each text page and give some references to explore further.

- **More stories.** I am limiting each concept to a single page, yet there are more and more stories—and I hope to continue to add to these tales. Live electrons are much easier to change than dead trees!

- **Your input.** Talking about how you and your community plan and get through changes can help others as well. So please join me there and add your stories and ideas as well.

Getting your community to plan together will strengthen relationships and make it possibe to adapt and thrive. So here is how to read this book to help your community plan matter what happens!

The most important thing we can do for our planet is to talk about the changes we are seeing.

While you do not have to go through every page, I suggest you use this book in a group for 8 sessions, one on each part, to plan within your community.

*Selfcareworldcare.wikidot.com/**dmdu** provides references for planning concepts.*

Introduction

The wicked problems out there are scary. You—and this workbook—can help your communities survive and thrive.

Why your community is here

Change does not have to be something that just happens TO us. We, too, can work for changes for the better: change can be an opportunity as well as a challenge. As Erin Brockovich (2021) says: "Think of each and every person in your community that you can help. Remember you just need enough confidence to take that first step in the right direction." We can understand and manage these transformations and plan and carry out robust solutions that will meet our needs and goals under a wide range of uncertain futures.

So what you and your community need now is something to help answer:

What the h*ll do we do now?

Communities need engagement and participation from everyone to plan and grow. You can use this book as part of a "book club" in your community—encouraging others to think through these ideas with you. You can use these very basic explanations as diving boards into much more in-depth studies and conversations at Selfcareworldcare.wikidot.com.

No matter who you are, you can be a voice to strengthen your community.

This guide and workbook is for you as:

- **A person who wants your community to thrive.** By encouraging your community to explore the concepts in this book, you can help people think about the future: What does this community truly value, and how can we support that no matter what happens in the future?

- **A leader and influencer in your community.** We are all leaders in a sense. As a leader, you can convey these concepts to others in your family, company, organization, and elsewhere—in other words, your spheres of influence, those groups you interact with. How could you lead to help your community thrive in these complex and ambiguous times?

- **A planner, coach, consultant, teacher, professor, scientist, academic.** So many books, journals, and more out there teach decision processes and talk about all of the complex problems today. This book gets the gist, the underlying zeitgeist, of these concepts to help you build a foundation for that planning.

Talk to people in your community. Who might be interested in helping your community thrive in the future?

This book explains how to embrace and transform the uncertainties and changes that face every hobby and interest (from hot air ballooning to canoeing to video gaming) and every community (from your family to a country halfway around the world). The concepts in this book and accompanying website, *Selfcareworldcare.wikidot.com* will get you and your community thinking about how to manage and transform change to become stronger, more vibrant, and more resilient.

Selfcareworldcare.wikidot.com/toc provides a list of all of the pages in this workbook as well as a list of other related concepts.

Why I wrote this for your community

Write what you know, the writing experts always say. On my first day on the job in 1991 as a Federal technical writer, my boss plonked down three huge black notebooks, with pages falling out and bindings cracked from an untold number of additions. "These are the Planning Instructions we follow," she told me. "Learn them and make sure that everything that comes through our reviewing process follow these." I went home crying that night. And every night for more than a week straight afterwards. Then, about a year later, President Clinton came on board and reinvented government—throwing most of the regulations out the window. We had secretaries standing by huge stacks of paper, showing just how many old and confusing Planning Instructions we had freed ourselves from. But the enginners complained bitterly and wanted specific guides for how to keep our infrastructure going and to ensure our mission happens in these changing and controversial times—when there were so many different and conflicted factions and voices?

We all need to understand the changes in the world now and how we can help transform those changes.

So, I, a very newbie writer, was drafted into creating a Decision Process. As I knew nothing, I just blithely interviewed people who did—folks building airports, introducing wolves, running a government agency, elected officials, and more—about 200 experts in all. These were all confidential (and I am sure the tapes we made just for writing up these insights were destroyed a long time ago), and I wrote up all of the advice in a neat little planning process. The agency used these concepts and processes and I continued to add to them.

My last planning guide process involved decision-making under deep uncertainty, which is a complex field of study all on its own—to answer: how can we plan when we don't know what the future will hold? This decision-making analysis uses many model runs to simulate what could happen under a wide range of possible futures and helps agencies determine what actions would help infrastructure and operations continue to function under these uncertain futures.

I examined government guides, scholarly books and articles, and examples of uncertainty planning in the government, academia, and private industry. So much is written on this that my reference list itself grew to over 50 pages! I am not going to bore you with all of these references because you can check the website, selfcareworldcare.wikidot. com for those.

But I am synthesizing these insights into this book for you to use in your own decision-making, and to share with others in your communities and your spheres of influence to help usall make better plans and decisions in these dynamic and uncertain times.

If we plan for change, we can make change work for us rather than against us.

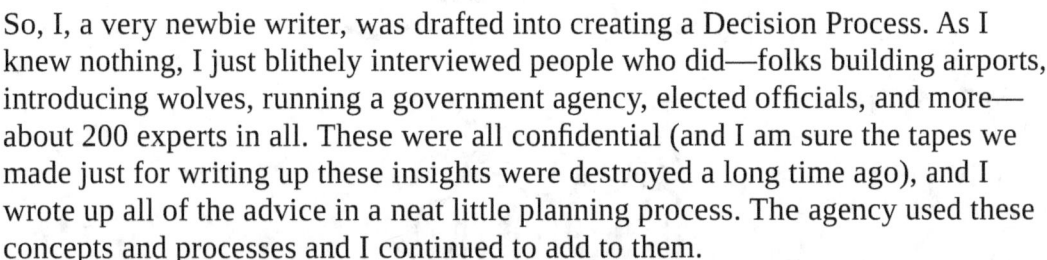

*Selfcareworldcare.wikidot.com/**dmdu** provides references for planning concepts.*

Part One:
Where are we in the change journey?

Ground and Center

Who are you journeying with?

Page: 3

Social and Ecosystems

How does your community work within the world?

Page: 5

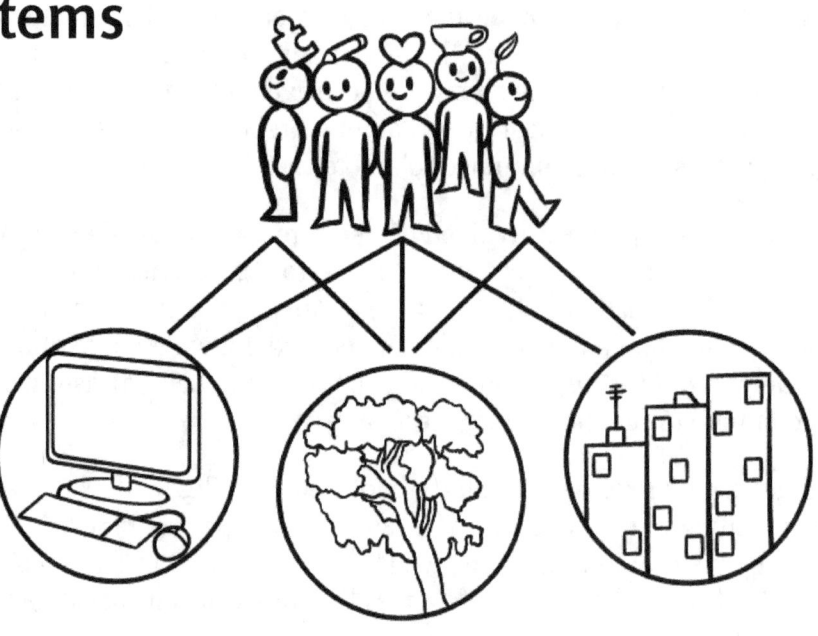

Recognizing Change

What are the changes in your world?

Page: 7

Accepting Change
How will we face changes in our communities?

Page: 9

Growth and Decay Cycle
What stages of change are your communities in?

Page: 11

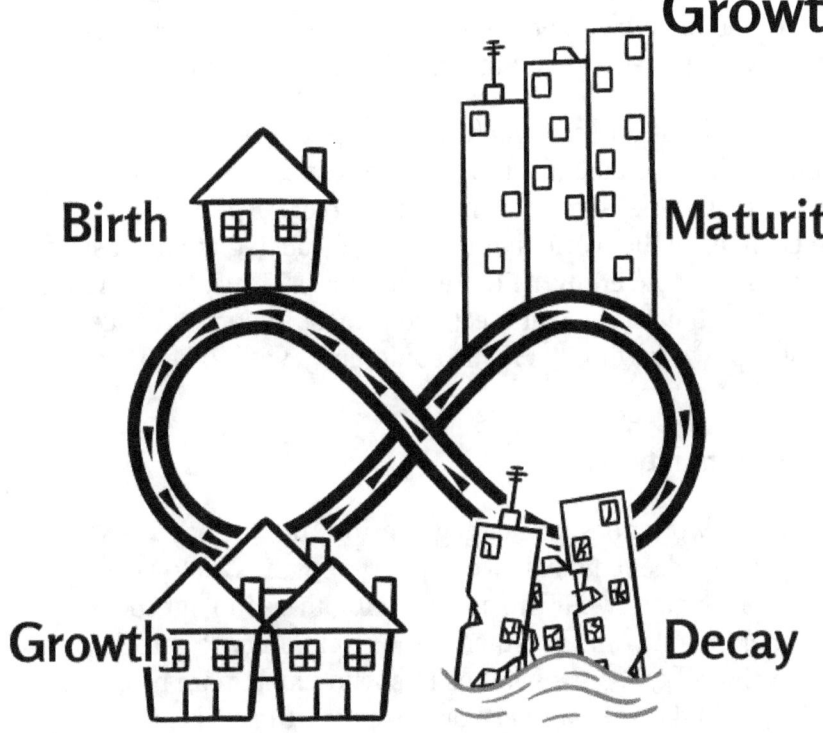

Traps
Where and why are we stuck?

Page: 13

Ground and Center

Communities form around similar interests and values. While the individual people differ, they come together to share beliefs and actions.

Who are you journeying with?

Identify your focus community—and get involved

We are each part of so many communities: your family, your buddies, people with similar interests, your neighbors, and beyond. And the people in these groups are all entangled in other networks and communities. All of these communities need to plan for how they will continue to work in uncertain futures. This book explains how your community can work together to determine what the community is all about and how to keep these essential functions working together.

However, you can't be involved in every group everywhere, nor can every group you are involved in engage in community planning to face common changes. Community action and planning is work, but it is worth it.

For this planning effort, focus on one of your many communities.

Focus your efforts. Do what you can where you can. Choose one or two of your communities that need the most love and attention now to face challenges together and to feel safer and more cohesive. Also look at your life—where are changes in the world and in your life causing the most stress? What issues are the most concerning? Figure out your priorities and commit to working just with a community that meets your most important concerns and priorities. You can work with this focus community with to help plan for a thriving future.

Build your focus community

This planning and care work does take engaged effort, but the payoffs will be well worth it: you can deepen your own support networks, help a cause you care about, and strengthen your life as you help others in your focus community. Spend enjoyable time together in the community to care for you and the community. Family therapists tell us to spend much more positive, quality time with a child than disciplinary or correcting time. The same may be true for building communities—how can you as a group come together?

Ground and center your focus community

Talk to people in your community. What are they concerned about? What are their issues?

Get engaged with your focus community—What are our needs and issues, and how can we work together to address these? Each community needs to be grounded in a common purpose and core identity — even when there are many arguments about that purpose. Work with others in your focus community to identify what that community is and why it is a community. Spark some group self reflection. You can ask:

- What makes this (family/neighborhood/community) what it is?
- What do we as a community need and value? What is essential to the function and survival of this community?

*Selfcareworldcare.wikidot.com/**groundworld**: Who are your communities and what is at the heart of your community?*

Which community will I focus on?

What are our shared interests, values, and needs?

Social and Eco Systems

How does your community work within the world?

Your focus community, the group you are working with to plan out your future, is not an isolated network. We are all part of an incredible number of interlocking social systems: family, community, town or city, county, state, nation, and world. When you can see yourself and your community as part of many interlocking systems—as part of the web of life on earth—you can better appreciate who you are and how you influence these systems. Rather than following or changing a single factor, we need to think about these how these interconnections form systems with many factors. There is not just a single thread or a single factor that changes everything—the overall systems rely on many factors to keep functioning.

Everything on Earth: people, society, the environment, and so on, all depend on each other in interlinked complex systems.

You and others in your focus community play a part within global economic and environmental systems: employers who need you to function, companies who want you to buy their products, banks that depend on your money to lend to others, and more. These social and economic systems depend on you, and you depend on them. In the same way, you are part of natural and physical systems. The water in your coffee has housed fish and other wildlife, grown forests and crops, flowed through generators to power your lights, made factories work, and so much more. Our ecosystems provides everything in our lives—from food and water to power and lights to clothes and transportation. We all live and rely on this one planet, Earth.

How can we work together to engage, inform and plan?

Think about the larger scale

And each of these systems work together on local to world scales: from family to world, from a tiny stream to a huge watershed, from a local rainstorm to a global weather pattern. Time scales also come into this, from quick changes to changes occurring over decades. Resources and possible changes happen differently at these various scales (just imagine if every family decision had to go through the same process as passing a law!).

Find your connections

See your actions as part of an interconnected whole. Understand and expand your spheres of influence.

Everyone in your focus community also has a wider sphere of influence—a different network of people and other communities they are connected with. Everyone knows someone. Who do you know? How can these connections work for your community? As part of a family, work, school, neighborhood, hobby, interest group, company, organization: connecting with one another is how we change ourselves, how we change others, and ultimately, how we change the world. That is your community's sphere of influence, your place in the world. You can expand or contract this, depending on who you reach out to and how you act. For example, you could put your government representatives in your contact list, start a twitter feed, join a group with your political outlook, run for office yourself, or find other contacts.

Selfcareworldcare.wikidot.com/connectworld: Your communities are interconnected with natural, social, physical, and economic systems.

Who / What does our community depend on?

Who / What depends on our community?

Recognizing Change

Changes can creep in gradually or erupt suddenly.

What changes are going on around your community?

If we plan for change, we can make change work for us rather than against us.

What are the changes in your world?

When my great grandmother came to America from Hungary in the 1840s, the voyage took three months. My grandmother only spent a few weeks to sail back to Europe before the first World War. My mother's crossing lasted less than a week when she went over after the second World War. And now my online conferences with colleagues from England, India, and New York take about 20 seconds for my internet to boot up and dial me in.

Some of these changes were gradual, and some were overnight—and usually it is a mix of the two. For example, Covid was a wave over the world in a few months, and changed business practices overnight, but the changes leading up to this worldwide epidemic (like air travel, cell phones, and global interdependence) took decades and longer. An earthquake can happen in a few second even though that stress had been building up for centuries.

Identify trends

Changes over a long period of time may not be seen every day, but we can pick out the general trends that may precede a sudden storm or shift in the world. Following the daily stock market changes may help day traders—but for those long-term investments like retirement, examine the changes over years and decades.

Talk about change

To handle change, we first have to acknowledge that everything does change and your community will either plan and manage that change or be surprised and scramble to keep functioning afterwards. Talk to each other about:

- What is your community's history? What major changes has your community undergone in the past? How were these handled? What can you learn from these experiences?

- What are the major causes of previous long-term change (urban growth, shifts in the economy, wars, natural disasters, etc.)

- What changes have been occurring over a long period of time (e.g., population, economy, jobs, ideas, cultures, education, technology)?

- How is your community embracing changing technologies, dealing with new weather patterns, welcoming new members with new ideas?

- What changes are anticipated in your community?

- What changes are projected over the next century and beyond? How will changing climates, sedimentation, population changes, and other factors affect your community?

Selfcareworldcare.wikidot.com/changeworld: Understanding the pace of change and recognizing change.

How has my community changed?

Accepting Change

The only thing we can control is how we approach and plan for constant change and uncertainty.

"We need to know we can fix it. To spur ourselves and each other to action we must provide a positive incentive to act, not just an apocalypse to avoid." Hayhoe 2021 page 82

Our world is going to change—no matter what. But together we can choose and direct our futures.

How will your community handle changes?

Change is happening all around the world—at a faster pace than ever before. Thousands of generations lived without plastics, pharmaceuticals, and other modern chemicals. Then within just a couple of generations, every organism on Earth has microplastics and chemicals swimming around in their cells. Cultural expectations have changed drastically with today's instant communication. How do people in your community handle these changes?

Denial won't work

Denying changes are happening will only make a few people richer for a while.

- **Pretending change does not exist.** For decades, tobacco companies pretended that second-hand smoke was not dangerous—they paid off a few scientists and created doubt when there really wasn't any—all we had to do was look at a few lung tissues. The same thing is happening in many other realms.

- **Pretending that one change would not cause a cascade of changes.** The Flint, Michigan planners who diverted the water supply from Detroit water to Flint River water did not allow for the inevitable corrosion and lead poisoning from this change. They did not think through these consequences, and many suffered.

- **Pretending that this is someone else's problem.** Now, sure, this "not in my backyard!" tactic may work for you personally, but changes are going to affect you and your community sooner or later—and probably sooner. That fire/flood/hail/storm insurance you should get? Yeah, it's gonna cost you a lot more now. That grocery bill? Yeah, it is going up as farms struggle with less water and more heat. Whatever hobby, job, family, whatever that you love—these changes will affect it.

Planning will work

- **Getting your community to recognize and face what is happening—and what could happen.** Understanding where your community has been, what changes have already happened, and what your community may face in the future can help you work together to plan.

- **Planning as a community to face changes.** There are many ways we as a community can address change, but really, the only one that will work is actively trying to understand and plan for these changes. Together, we can affect the future, we can manage the transitions—we can be the dynamic heroes. We can expand the coping range, plan the transformation, and find robust solutions.

Selfcareworldcare.wikidot.com/acceptworld: Storytelling and preserving the past can provide insights into the future.

How do people in my community cope with change?

Growth and Decay Cycle

Communities go through cycles of change, but different facets will be at different stages.

These cycles of change are at every level: from your neighborhood to the world.

Determine where your community is so you can plan how changes may happen and what you can do.

What stages of change are the people, systems, and institutions in your communities in?

Everything: every life, environmental and economic system, organization, and institution goes through a cycle of emergence, birth, growth, and decay/disruptive change into a new system, when the cycle starts all over again. Think about your neighborhood—which emerged and grew to meet the needs of people moving in, solidified into streets and houses and properties, and is now hard to change. Or a tiny company or even nation that starts out fast and furious—able to do anything, to grow into an established process, to mature into hardfast rules and inflexible infrastructure and complex bureaucracy, and then can't adapt and must radically transform. You can work within each of these stages to protect and grow your community's core values and functions:

- **Birth:** The community is reorganizing from a destructive event or a collapsing system and newly emerging from new technologies or possbilities. What is this new effort trying to address? How can you help guide this effort to meet these needs and objectives? How can you partner with others to get the resources needed for this new beginning? How can your community use changing technologies in new ways?

- **Growth:** The community is still beginning and establishing. How will you recognize the new system and what objectives for robust strategies do you need to help manage this transformation? To work with these, be creative about what can happen, what you can do, and what would you like the system to do as it emerges.

- **Maturity:** The community has invested and grown a certain way and is now less flexible to adapt to changes. What are the tipping points and what innovative approaches can help avoid traps and create more flexibility to adapt to changes to avoid tipping points? Most of our systems today are mature to the point where we need to nudge the system rather than remake the system. Infrastructure like buildings and roads or even cars or tractors can't be easily moved or torn down for a wide scale change. Transforming this past investment requires flexible approaches within the system so that we can manage change without falling into chaos. And yet, even attitudes set in stone can change. Think about how attitudes towards women working, marijuana use, interracial marriage, and other issues have changed drastically. This same sea change of attitudes can happen even within our most mature mindsets.

- **Decay:** The community can no longer function as it had. It is crossing a tipping point into a new system. How can you maintain resources within these dramatic changes? How can we plan for the next regime shift? Keep checking in with people, institutions, and systems in your community to see what is in which stage of these interlocking cycles.

Selfcareworldcare.wikidot.com/cycleworld: More ideas on working within each stage to adapt to changes.

Birth

Maturity

Growth

Decay

What stages are people in our community in?

Traps

Recognizing when something is stuck and why it is stuck is the first step in getting going again.

Work together to recognize and escape traps.

Periodically review: has your community fallen into a trap?

Where and why are we stuck?

Identifying traps can be tough when you are in one. We can't do this because we need that. But to get that, we need to have already done this!

Community actions and solutions often bog down in traps—but the traps may not be obvious at first glance. Watch out for these!

- **Hopelessness trap.** Sometimes it feels like the world is just going to collapse no matter what we do. That the tipping point has already been reached. And the "why bother/let it rot"? sets in. This fear and hopelessness is understandable and totally ok. But your community will flounder and end sooner if you just give up. *Escape: Do something, anything, and see what effect it has. Planting a community garden or posting a free library can spark a reaction throughout your change net.*

- **Poverty trap.** If kids need to hike on a barely-there trail through deserts or jungles to get to school, then come home and hike more to get their family's water, the daylight hours disappear—and they can not study, and the community continues to suffer in this poverty trap: you need resources to get resources. *Escape: band with other communities in the same situation and pool resources, ask for resources.*

- **Maintenance trap.** The beautiful new well in the village breaks—and then how can it be fixed? Parts are too expensive or too far away, and the well is now a broken shell—and the long arduous water walks begin again. There are no teachers to teach in the new school building, so the long hikes to school resume. *Escape: Address the original problem again but this time, scout out what could go wrong and have a plan to continue the actions (can someone in the village can fix the well?).*

When you work in a community, there are some other traps you can fall into:

- **Nothing about us without us!** Groups will resent outsiders, and outsiders will have different ideas that groups may not agree with. And even then, each member of the group will have a different perspective. You really do need to involve everyone who cares.

- **Everyone has to agree!** No, they don't. You do need a common purpose and a commitment to work together. You can find common ground, something everyone is concerned about and needs. Consensus may not be possible—but understanding the need for the action and consenting to it may be. (Ok, I don't agree, but I see why we need this!)

- **Analysis Paralysis!** Sometimes sending things to a committee to study is just avoiding the commitment to act. Deciding to delay is a decision to not act at all. So find a no or low regret action you can do now.

---

*Selfcareworldcare.wikidot.com/**trapworld**: More types of traps and more ways to get out of them.*

Where is our community stuck?

Part Two:
How can you understand change?

Information

What information can we use about our world?

Page: 17

Change Network

How does change create more change in an interconnected world?

Page: 18

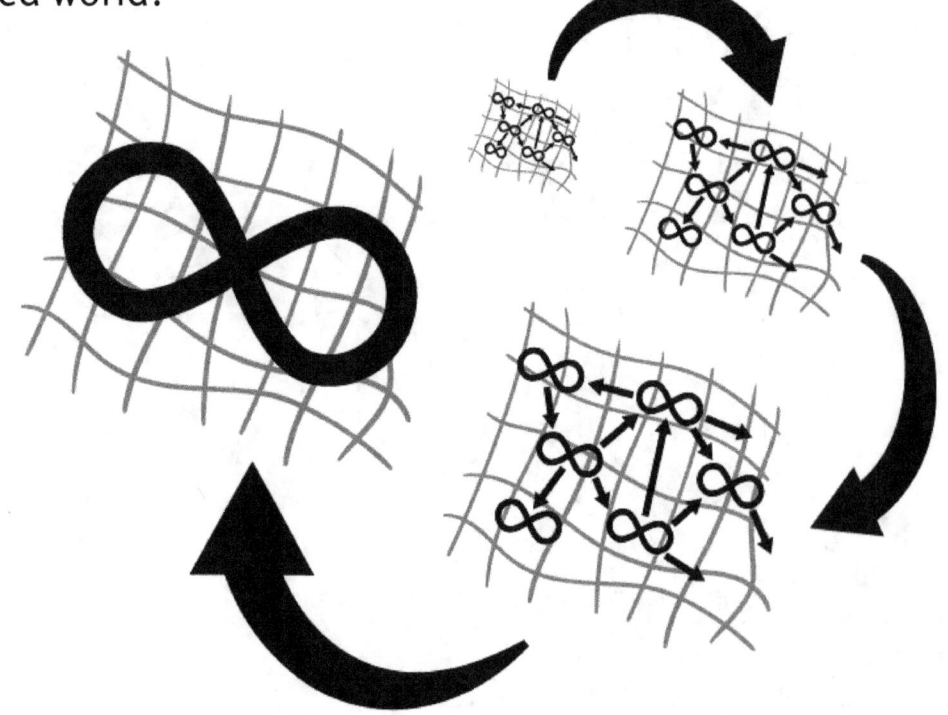

Wicked Problems

How can we address tangled, messy problems?

Page: 19

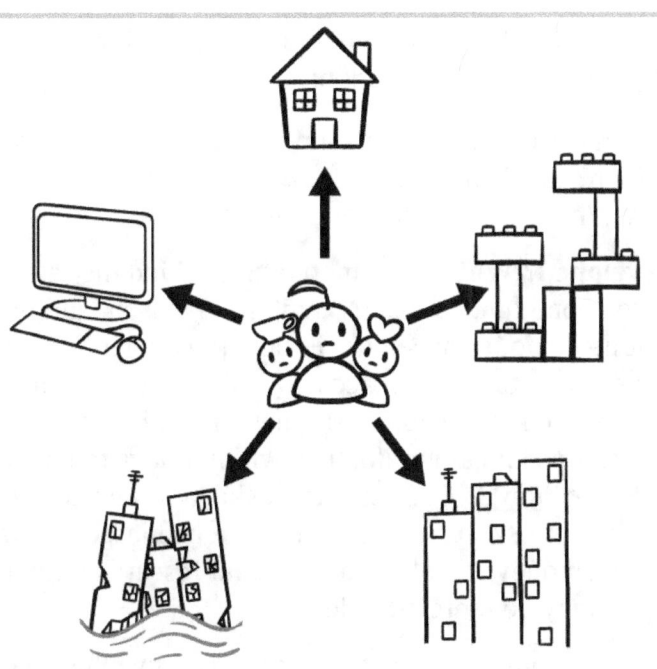

Deep Uncertainty

How can we prepare for what we don't know?

Page: 21

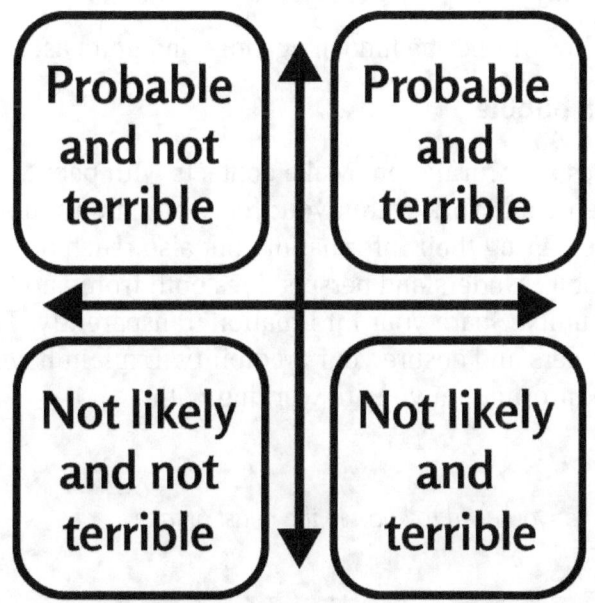

Vulnerability and Risk

Where could communities break down?

Page: 23

Information

Investigate the information sources and determine what sources are reliable.

Reach beyond your own information bubble.

Try to find new perspectives and question information sources.

What information can we use about our world?

We exist in a drowning flood of information coming from so many firehoses at once. You don't have time to check out every source and understand every wicked problem—you don't even have time to actually read those long-winded agreements you signed when you opened up the software. Even the form of information changes ever more rapidly: it took centuries to go from horses to the telegraph, decades to go from telegraph to radio to television to the internet, and now almost no time to go from one social media platform to whatever comes next this week. You don't have time to check out who is sending you the information or what their agenda is.

Acting on misinformation quickly can just make the situation worse. So you need to do your own research. Check with a lot of information sources, not just one. **Slow down. Think through what you just found out.**

Get the facts first and then decide how to act on that information. Use information wisely. Question your information:

- **Where is it coming from?** If one person wrote it, where did that person get the information? Is this their opinion or is it based on studies? What is this based on? What else have they written?

- **Why was it developed?** What is the motivation behind the research? If this is a study, someone funded this research for a reason, and often this reason can be quite devious and subtle. Follow the money. Who benefits from the findings? For example, tobacco companies developed their own research and sowed confusion over whether smoking is harmful. If industry can prove a chemical is safe, they will not have to pay to clean up the chemical or to stop using it and start using a more expensive process. So the industry-sponsored research may be biased and faulty as there is so much money at stake. Independent research without the money on the line may be more reliable.

- **How old is this information?** New discoveries and insights change older information. So stay up to date as much as you can.

- **Read the fine print.** You'll find the hidden agendas and gotchas!

Get out of your information bubble

Get a diverse array of sources of information. Make contacts with people who have differing ideas than you. Work within your focus community to understand where people are getting their information, but also reach out beyond that information bubble. Understand perspectives both from and outside of your focus community. Share your information transparently. This is critical to engage stakeholders and ensure your credibility. Explain how, where, and why you got the information you are working with.

Selfcareworldcare.wikidot.com/infoworld: Find what you need to know in the midst of fake news and information bubbles and verify sources.

- Where do we get information?
- How can we verify these sources?
- How can we share verified information?

Change Network

Recognizing how changes and processes are interconnected helps us understand causes and effects in complex systems.

Changes occur at all community levels.

Trace out the ripple effects of one change in your community.

How does one change create more changes in an interconnected world?

Changes in one place cause changes in other places, which then can lead to more and more effects over time. Often, the changes you see in your community not only create other changes but have deeper root causes. Tracing this "change network" can help focus solutions and predict other changes. Trace these effects and ask:

- What causes these changes? How do other system parts change along with these changes? Do the following changes affect the original change, making effects even more deeper and even more intense?

- What depends on this resource that is changing? How do these changes affect other factors, resources, etc.?

What changes at other scales do we need to consider?

A minor change can lead to further changes within the same resource or factor. Follow the change network and ask:

- What will change in the future? How will the infrastructure and operations work under these changes?

- What will still function in a range of dynamic changes? What won't function?

- How has your focus community developed? What major changes has your community undergone in the past?

Think through feedback loops

Changes can reverberate through a change net and loop back to cause more changes in the original change. For example, if water is scarce during a drought, the air gets drier and hotter, decreasing the chance for clouds to form and to get rain. Plants can die off and leave dust and erosion, which can lead to faster runoff. Snow can melt more quickly, and thus snowmelt runs off faster with less time for water to soak into the ground. Less groundwater leaves less water for plant roots and the cycle of plants dying and water runoff continues to get even worse.

Think at different scales

Systems range in scale from local patches of habitat to a wider ecosystem, from a stream to a watershed to a basin, from a neighborhood to a nation. Changes ripple across on many levels: from a local community to a global economic and environmental system. Be aware of where your changes are taking place and the levels above and below your focus community.

Selfcareworldcare.wikidot.com/**changenetwork**: *How to trace cascading changes and feedback loops.*

local

regional

What changes

affect our

national

community?

global

Wicked Problems

How can we address tangled, messy problems?

Wicked problems are complex with many causes, many solutions, and many perspectives.

You've all heard it—in a barbershop, at a family dinner, everywhere from a little league game to talking (or shouting) heads on a TV show. Everyone knows exactly how to solve the complex, intertangled, and downright perplexing problems of our day: from poverty and homelessness to wars and revolutions, from energy crises to climate change. Yet if their great and easy ideas were put into practice, would the problems really be solved? Probably not. Wicked problems, caused by many processes and conditions, influence many processes and lives. They need an interconnected community to solve them, and there won't ever be a simple approach, a single answer. Wicked problems are intertwined into our existing, mature economic, social and cultural, technical, environmental, and legal systems.

The more wicked the problem, the more people and groups we need involved to solve it.

Addressing one element of one problem will probably cause some other element to change as well—unintended consequences abound when attacking wicked problems. For example, New York City solved the high rent problem by freezing rents. But this led to maintenance declines and then property values decreased. A one-child policy in China lead to a population decrease, but now there are fewer workers to support the large number of retirees. You do have to think through the consequences of actions for wicked problems.

To address these complex problems, we need to first understand as much as we can about them and how they affect your community:

- **Follow one thread.** Just as you untangle threads by following one end backwards, do the same here. Find one specific issue, and work backwards: What is the problem? What are the underlying causes?

- **Get as many perspectives as possible**. The more input from the more perspectives you have, the less precarious your predictions and foresight and solutions will be. This does involve working with people with agendas and goals and beliefs that are different from yours. But a wide range of explanations for the problems will help us all see different aspects and come up with new solutions. Ask people in—and out of—your focus community.

As a group, take one aspect of a problem facing your community and brainstorm backwards: What are the causes? And then forwards: what are the effects?

- **Think about entire ecosystems and processes.** One simple aspect is not enough. For example, just recycling glasses and cans will not address the pollution or resources problems we face. Recycling needs to think about cradle to cradle—how could our products be created, used, recycled, and used again in a systematic way?

You can't just give up, nor can you test your solution. You have to do something, monitor what you did, and then adjust.

Selfcareworldcare.wikidot.com/wickedworld: Examine the many reasons these issues are complex.

What wicked problems are we facing?

Who else is affected?

Can we work on these together?

Deep Uncertainty

Deep uncertainty occurs when participants in a decision process do not know or cannot agree on how the future will look.

We don't have to agree on what the future will bring—we need to consider many possible futures and be prepared for change and managed transformations.

Explore what could happen—and plan solutions that will work for a wide range of possible futures.

How can we prepare for what we don't know?

Planners call situations where decision makers and stakeholders do not know or cannot agree on how likely different futures may be "deep uncertainties." We live in deep uncertainty, where no one can agree on what the future will hold. We never really know something completely, thoroughly, and unchanging forevermore. Inevitably, the more we study something, the more we understand that there is a lot more we don't understand. Acknowledging the surprise factor in everything will help prepare uncertainties. As we find out more, we can change to handle the new information and new ideas.

Understand what we don't understand

It takes some humility to know that we don't know everything about a situation or how the future will unfold. It is easier to think that we do have enough information. However, we don't know even the extent of what we don't know (the unknown unknowns). For example, is there an alien life form in the galaxy, and if so, what is their equivalent of our coffee? Not only do we not know who that might be or if they would have the same senses as us, we don't know their social structures, interconnected ecosystems, etc. Thus we aren't even aware of what to ask about this alien race! Closer to home, we discover thousands of new species on earth every year. We need to plan for these unknown factors that lurk outside what we know.

We don't know what will happen.

We do need to create the plans before we know what will really happen. How will humans behave in the future? What will our planet look like? We really don't know—but the good news is that we don't have to kow everything to plan. Uncertainties stem from the limits or lack of evidence or information. We may not know enough to untangle all of the complex interrelationships between animals and plants and water and climate. Scientists understand these limitations, acknowledge the uncertainty, and adjust results as new information or evidence comes in. We have limited time and resources to study these complex relationships, and cannot study everything.

We don't know what we don't know

There are many "flavors" or levels of uncertainty:

- Things we know (but we could be wrong)
- Things we don't know (and it would take a lot to find out)
- Things we aren't even aware of what we don't know (that we don't even know enough to ask these questions, let alone explore answers).

*Selfcareworldcare.wikidot.com/**uncertaintyworld**: what is uncertain and how to handle uncertainty in our communities.*

What uncertainties do we face?

Vulnerability and Risk

Where could communities break down?

Look at the weakest links to see where communities are likely to fail. The more your community can strengthen these weaker points, the more your community can survive and thrive. Vulnerability measures how easily a resource, asset, or user could be damaged by a change to the point where the community will undergo a regime shift, that is to collapse and emerge as something new as the growth/decay cycle continues. Risk is how likely these threat are and how much damage would be done if that threat became reality.

These are areas where the community may fail, and projections for how likely that failure may be.

What is vulnerable in your focus community?

Think about the weakest links that your community interacts with (either in the environment, economy, or social network). Vulnerability depends on:

- **Exposure.** What is stressing your community? What problems could we face, how bad could these be, and how long would they last (e.g., how long a drought lasts and how severe it is).

- **Sensitivity.** How well can your community handle that stress? How fragile is that factor and how many resources are there to withstand that problem (e.g., how much do we depend on rain?).

- **Adaptive capacity.** How much can your community change to cope with the problem (e.g., using different water sources during a drought).

What could cause a tipping point where the community changes structure and function?

Who is vulnerable in your community?

When considering risks, consider those who would be most affected by those events both within your community and in the larger economic and environmental systems connected with your community. The poor and minorities are often more affected by changes than others. For example, the poor can't afford to move to a location without frequent hurricanes or rising sea levels, and even when the hurricanes or floods come, they can't afford to evacuate as they may not have transportation or shelter where they could go even if they could leave. Minorities have often been denied fair housing in the past, forcing them to live in communities with higher levels of pollution.

How likely is failure—and what would be the consequences?

Assessing risks by asking how likely is the change to occur and how much of an impact would that change have. Think about both the short and long term:

- How does this change relate to vulnerabilities inherent in your community?

- Can the community recover from this change?

Work with people in and outside your community to identify weak points and potential problems.

Selfcareworldcare.wikidot.com/riskworld: what and who are vulnerable and how to manage risks.

Who
Where are our weakest areas?
What

Part Three:
How do we track changes?

Indicators

How can we track warning signs in the world?

Page: 29

Resilience

How well can our community recover?

Page: 31

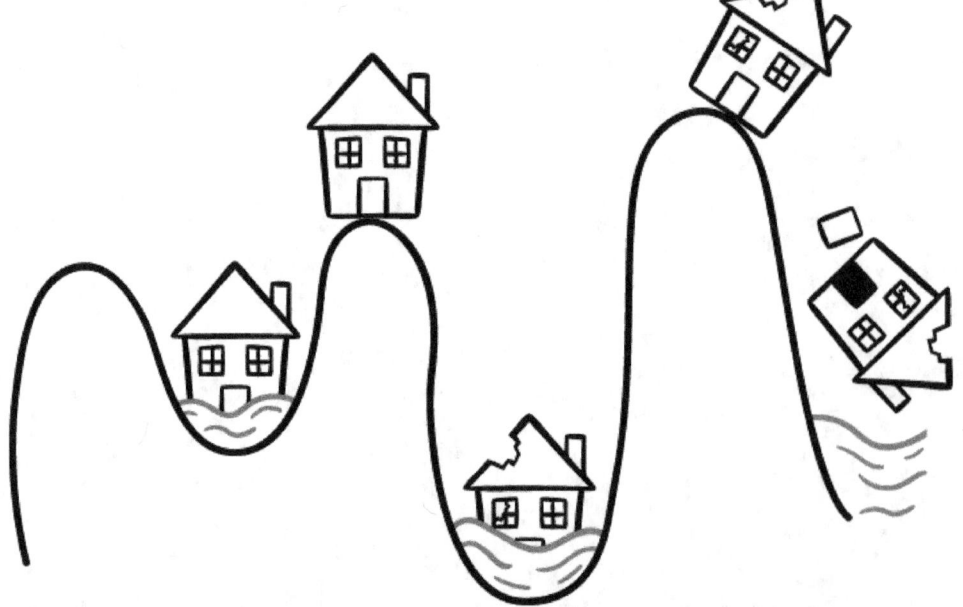

Coping Range

How can we expand what our community can handle?

Page: 33

Tipping Points

When does our community fail and transform into something new?

Page: 35

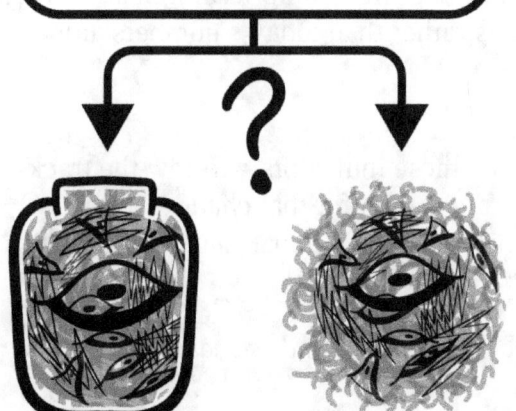

Regime Shifts

How can we manage these new systems?

Page: 37

Indicators

Indicators are relatively small, measurable key factors that generally reflect impacts for an overall issue or community.

Indicators help you know when to sound the alarm.

How can we track warning signs in the world?

You can't watch everything in every ecosystem and interconnected network at the same time. Ok, you can not ever keep track of so much! Select a particular factor that could show what is happening overall. Think of these as the canaries in the coal mines (if the canary passed out, the air was bad). Indicators should be:

- **Relevant:** What are the connections between the sign and your focus community? Food bank participation can show economic conditions.

- **Available and measurable:** Can we get comparable data to analyze? Food banks can be compared in different cities, but data may differ.

- **Reliable**. Can we get consistent information over time? Food banks that have been around can provide histories.

- **Leading:** What will be affected first? Where are weak spots?

Search for signs

Look around your community: are there signs of trouble? Go back to the communities' discussions of weak points and vulnerability—what are some warning signs you can watch? For example:

- Economic signs may be an increase in food bank use, evictions, etc.

- Unusual signs like many people with the same unusual health issues in the same area may signal a problem in the environment.

- The presence of an endangered species that depends on a certain environment can be an indicator for an entire ecosystem's health.

Track these signs

Find out if there are other cases with similar changes in warning signs. For example, Dr. Mona Hanna-Attisha accessed children's medical records in Flint Michigan and determined that blood lead levels had nearly doubled after Flint changed from the Detroit water to Flint River water.

Watch over a long period to see long-term gradual trends. Note that daily or even monthly fluctuations are does not track long-term trends—look at years worth of stock market returns rather than today's numbers alone.

Analyze these signs

Work with universities, planners, non-profit agencies and others to determine which indicators to use and how to interpret these numbers.

Look for interrelationships between these indicators—follow the tracks backward to measure change and the causes for that change. These indicators will help you measure your action's impacts and plan what to do when (adaptive pathways).

selfcareworldcare.wikidot.com/indicatorworld: Choosing indicators and understanding their benefits.

What conditions would raise an alarm?

What will give us an idea of where the system is going?

Resilience

Resilience is the ability for a system to withstand, adapt to, and recover from stresses and shocks.

How well can our community recover?

Hurricane Cthulhu comes roaring into your town. Power is out for days, streets flood, trash piles up, diseases proliferate. How can our communities recover? Storms, droughts, plagues, and more—how much change or disruption can your community, our social and ecological systems handle while still being the same system? No single approach will work for all communities—but we all need to plan for resilience before, during, and after.

Before the storm

- **Assess and prepare for risks.** Recognize potential sudden and gradual threats to your community: What could happen? Then prepare, plan, monitor, and adapt. Think about the overall economic and environmental systems your community is connected to.

- **Understand and monitor gradual situations.** Consciously tracking indicators and using these indicators to analyze overall systems can help predict what may happen and help to prepare.

- **Determine ways to make your community more resilient.** How can we manage healthy changes? Find flexible and adaptable plans, with back ups and redundant systems that help withstand future storms.

Systems may not be able to return to the same state after a stress.

During the storm

While it is hard to think in the middle of the storm, work together to cooperate and share resources to survive the crises. Note your ideas and struggles. Take pictures if you can to remind others how severe storms can be.

After the storm

Think about the big picture:

- **Who has been left behind?** Not everyone has the same chances to recover. People with lower incomes, people of color, the unhoused, and the disabled may face the harshest impacts from these storms and may not have the resources needed to recover from disasters as quickly. How can we support these communities?

- **How can we build in more resilience?** Improve systems after the stress by asking what can we do now to adapt to the stress if it happens again? For example, not rebuilding in a flood or fire zone may be an option. Or build to withstand future wildfires.

- **How can we manage graceful failures?** It may not be possible to rebuild a community or to keep a community going. Managing a new system into a regime shift may need to be considered.

Set up communication networks to strengthen your community before emergencies happen.

*Selfcareworldcare.wikidot.com/**resilienceworld**: how to plan before storms, support your community during storms, and manage these tipping points.*

What can help us bounce back?

Coping Range

A community can only function within a certain range. Actions can help expand that range

Helping others expands your coping range as well.

How can you expand coping ranges to function in more extreme conditions than in the past?

How can we expand what our community can handle?

Everything: all of us, and our communities, ecosystems, economic systems, etc. has a coping range—what we can handle and what conditions will overwhelm us and shift into a new regime (transform to a new system). Be aware of these coping ranges so that we can understand and manage transitions for your focus community. Knowing the coping range and what affects that range may lead to identifying actions that could expand that coping range. "Levers" is another term planners use for these actions.

Many factors go into determining these coping ranges. For example, coffee plants grow best when temperatures are between 64 and 70 degrees Fahrenheit (°F) (17 to 21 degrees Celsuis (°C). Coffee plants can actually tolerate a little bit more heat than this. But a berry borer and a fungus that attack coffee plants also thrive in warmer conditions, and these pests have spread to almost all coffee-producing regions. So warmer conditions will harm the plants. Moreover, most farmers producing coffee barely survive now—let alone if their crops fail. Thus, a few bad years could put the farmers and their families out of business. After that, you might not be able to wake up and smell the coffee in the morning. However, if we examine the coffe plant's coping range and consider all the associated environmental and economic systems needed to get from the plant to your cup, we can find ways to expand coffee's coping range, such as developing shaded coffee plantations, attacking pests, selecting hardier coffee plants, and supporting farmers.

Use systems planning and look at the big picture as you determine your focus community's coping ranges and how we can expand these coping ranges and the larger systems connected to it. Some ways to expand these ranges are to:

- **Develop communication and support networks:** Trusted networks provide ways for everyone to help before an emergency. Searching for lost dogs practices searching for lost people

- **Consider the thresholds:** How long can your community handle stresses if they go on for a long time or if they become more severe? What are your tipping points?

- **Work with weak areas**: Where are your community's vulnerabilities and risks? What is likely to fail? What can be done to strengthen those areas?

- **Work with strong areas:** What works well? How can we spread that success?

Strengthening the people, institutions, ecosystems, etc. in your focus community now will help communities thrive no matter what happens.

Selfcareworldcare.wikidot.com/copeworld: how to expland your coping range and do what works for your community.

How can we increase our coping range?

What can we handle now?

Tipping Points

When does our community fail and transform something new?

Tipping points are the times when your community may not be able to continue as it is and will change. These can be planned changes (like a large company opening in the community) or unplanned (like a company declaring bankruptcy and laying off all workers). When a larger system like an environmental or economic system does not have the resiliency to recover, a new system emerges (regime shift). The transition can be triggered by a something sudden like a wildfire or flood, or a something slow and almost unnoticed like the social phenomenon of change from smoking being allowed and encouraged everywhere to smoking being banned from nearly everywhere. An individual event can bring slowly simmering issues to a boil and trigger a large change, erupting in protests like Black Lives Matter when too many individual tragedies have been more than enough to take action.

Tipping points can also occur in your community's mindset. The second dancer or hundredth monkey theories show that when enough people embrace an idea, then that becomes mainstream—and people act. The more people convinced of an idea, the closer the community gets to a tipping point and changes.

Managing Tipping Points

Review the weak points, or vulnerabilities in your community. Use your indicators—at what point could these weak points break? It is impossible to measure the precise tipping point, so you will need to build in a safety margin.

Do you want your community to reach that point? It might be ok to transform or it might be catastrophic. The further steps in this workbook will help set up a "what if" adaptive path plan to help your community plan to prevent reaching that point and what to do if systems come close that point. But first, it is vital to recognize that your community could tip and change—and ask if this current community is worth keeping:

- What are our tipping points and how can we avoid reaching them or plan for reaching them (see Regime Shift)?
- How will overall systems change? How will your community's goals and objectives change under a range of these possible future changes?
- What are your community's robust goals: what needs to continue to function in your community—no matter what?
- What is the minimum needed to function under changing conditions?
- At what points will more actions and analysis be needed to support these values and performance priorities?

Tipping points are transitions that happen when your community cannot continue in its current form.

When will your community shift into something new?

Ask people in your community about possible tipping points for your community and interconnected systems.

Selfcareworldcare.wikidot.com/tipworld: How to identify and manage tipping points.

What are our past tipping points?

Where might our community tip?

Regime Shifts

When your community goes beyond its coping range and does not have the resilience to bounce back from a problem, the community shifts into a new way of doing things.

Either we plan for something new or something new emerges on its own.

What can your community do to manage these transformations?

How can we manage the new systems?

When tipping points are reached and the larger interconnected system or your focus community can not revert back to what it was before the stress, it changes into something new. This is the decay and birth portion of the growth/decay cycle, and it happens at every level from the smallest organism to the biggest galaxy.

Planners call this a "regime shift" as we can acknowledge what is lost and transform into a new system. Think of managing the new situation as a graceful failure, a smooth transition into something new. As a community, we need to acknowledge and understand this shift so that we can manage in the new system and new circumstances. We can plan for handling a system regime shift, for example, replanting tree species further up the mountain so that they will grow up in an ecosystem that they can thrive in, even as the climate warms.

Graceful failures provide opportunity for reflection

As a community, we need to analyze the changes that these larger systems are going through and re-examine our objectives.

- How can our objectives change to meet the new realities?
- How can we manage within the new realities to meet objectives?

These questions will take a lot of work for your focus community—as much or even more than getting the community objectives in the first place. But having a conscious discussion helps acknowledge the changes the system has gone through—whether it is a gradual change that is now very apparent or a sudden event.

Change that provides an opportunity for action

Whenever there is a big traumatic, dramatic change, first look at how we can use this change to rebuild and improve the system. The world is mostly in the mature phase, where we have had a few centuries of infrastructure development that is hard to just sweep away. But disruptions to this infrastructure can provide rare opportunities (action moments) to improve processes—we just have to think about these issues and be ready to pounce.

Manage the transformation

How can we prepare for these radical changes? What does the community want to see as new ways to cope with the changes that have happened? How can you get there? What can you plan and do now and in the future to shape this new interconnected system and to prepare your community?

Selfcareworldcare.wikidot.com/regimeworld: Manage graceful failures, protect vulnerable factors, and rebuild after a regime shift.

What new
futures can
we plan?

What could
we do after
a cataclysmic
change?

Part Four:
How can we plan for uncertain futures?

Action Moments

How can we prepare for opportunities to act?

Page: 41

Systems Planning

How can we think about these interconnected communities and processes?

Page: 43

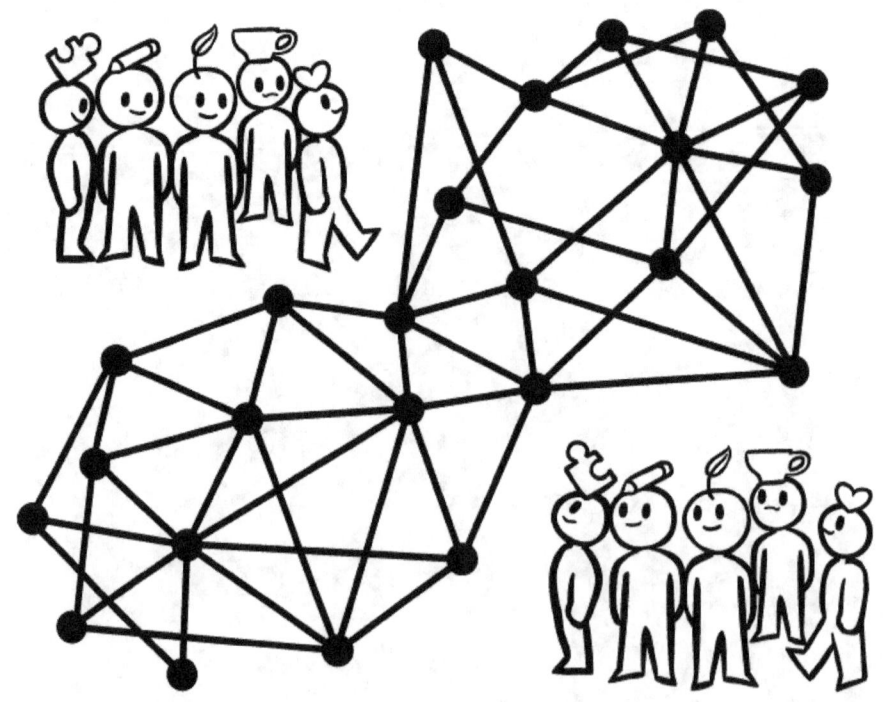

Scenarios

What wide range of futures can we imagine?

Page: 45

Resources

What can our community use?

Page: 47

Constraints

What can't our community do?

Page: 49

Action Moments

Action moments are opportunities when change can happen.

How can we prepare for opportunities to act?

When opportunity knocks, or when sudden changes happen, you want to be ready to take advantage of the new situation to direct and manage that new situation. Planning ahead of time to understand basic needs and brainstorm different ways to meet those needs can help make change happen when circumstances allow for this managed change

Create visions for transformations

Unless you know beforehand how you want to adapt the future and manage the transformations, you won't be able to do much when the time comes and you could miss that chance. So spending time envisioning the future as a community brings communities together, provides a foundation for change, and creates a direction to focus that change. For example, managing forests after a raging wildfire could take various forms: from controlling erosion to determining what kind of vegetation would be best to restore. If people know about and consent to (or even support!) a plan to manage forests if there is a fire ahead of time, then that plan can be put in place immediately after the fire—rather than having to wait afterwards to get people together to determine a plan for this regime shift

Keep plans ready so you can act quickly when the time is right.

Explain why actions are needed

Just asking someone to change won't work—and even more so with a community of people! People take action when they understand the reasons for doing so, and where these reasons resonate with their concerns. Find the interface that meets where people are emotionally. Talk about the underlying values and the value their actions would have. But these talks take a lot of time and it is better to do all of this thinking before the tipping point, before the regime shift. That way, we can move quickly after an event (like rebuilding with stronger infrastructure to prevent future flooding).

Take advantage of stress to change

Existing, mature infrastructure is often difficult to change. But sometimes events make it possible to change these established systems. For example, planners in Culver City, California, were helping their community envision a new grid for transportation, as this is the Los Angeles traffic hub. But streets and bus routes were set in stone and difficult to change—until Covid hit. With the lower traffic and the need to create outdoor dining spaces, there was enough momentum to change some of the transportation infrastructure. Emergencies and disasters can be a time to rebuild better. Droughts can be an opportunity to pass laws permitting (or even requiring) using native plants and stones for landscapes to avoid wasting water on green lawns. Power shortages can encourage people to put solar panels on their roofs.

How can we plan now to take advantage for future moments when change is possible?

*Selfcareworldcare.wikidot.com/**actworld**: how to empower people, grab opportunities, and take advantage of crises.*

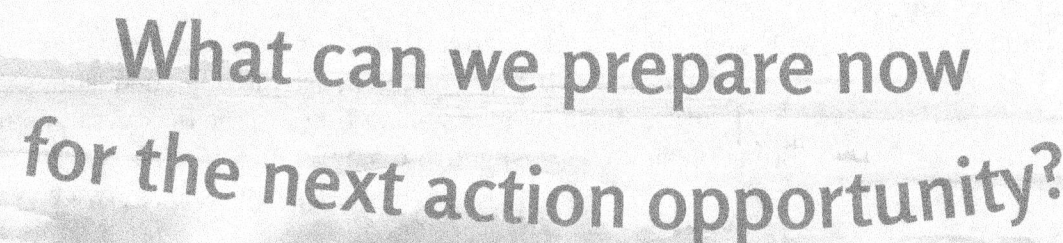

What can we prepare now for the next action opportunity?

Systems Planning

How can we think about these interconnected systems?

As you start to think about ways that your focus communities could prepare for a range of futures, use a big-picture approach to get the context you need to work within these interconnected change nets. No one acts alone in a vacuum—our actions not only change our lives, but what we do and say changes others, too.

What is changing?

Understanding the entire system allows us to see how changes to one part will affect the whole. It isn't enough to see the interconnections and links—we have to step outside the system at times to see the overall picture. Getting information about the system from many sources helps us see the whole and how your community's actions will affect the whole, and vice versa.

For example, ecosystems have closed loops: what is waste for one species is food for another. As a tree dies, fungi and other plants grow on it, and animals feed on those plants, and animal waste fertilizes the next generation of trees. If one part of this process changes, the rest will too. So follow the entire change net to see how one change will affect others. Watch your indicators to help recognize changes.

What are the root causes?

Oh, the why stage of a toddler. Everything is why, why, why? But these young'uns instinctively know that we need to find out the root causes. You can map backwards with these whys: What is the change? Why is it happening? Addressing root causes is more effective than working with symptoms. These will be wicked problems, and there will be more than one cause, so again, try to see as much of the big picture as you can.

How can individual actions influence the whole community?

Individuals acting by themselves may not make much of an impact, but many individuals acting together could. If you can see your individual action works within a system of actions, you can gather power. Something might seem small, like protesting or writing a letter to a company or to your congress person. For example, landscaping your own backyard to save water may not make a huge impact in a city's water supply, but if you could influence a neighbor to do the same, and that neighbor talks to someone else, you soon start a chain reaction. If enough people join in, water conservation could help a city weather that drought.

To work together, people in your focus community need a shared image of the system they are in. Work with others both in and outside of your community to find these causes and help to see the whole picture.

Taking a big picture mindset to planning allows us to address influences and find more effective solutions.

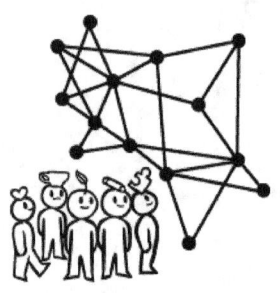

We are all on the same planet, all in the same boat. A hole in one part of the boat can sink the entire boat.

Describe and share your vision, and get perspectives from others. Note their issues as well.

Selfcareworldcare.wikidot.com/**systemworld**: *how to see the whole as well as the parts.*

What systems do we intersect with?

Scenarios

We can imagine a set of futures and plan for those.

What wide range of futures can we imagine?

Scenario planning spins stories of what might happen in the future so that you can imagine how your actions and options will work under a wide range of futures.

What could happen in the future?

Creating stories about the future is a basis for planning for everything from financial markets and economic conditions to water availability. Experts in many fields create models to simulate what would happen in these futures to help examine possible outcomes and develop possible strategies to cope.

Modelers may have time and resources to run many different future scenarios to find exactly what the signposts and tipping points are and exactly how an option will work under a wide range of potential futures. You probably don't have that luxury. However, at the very least, think of a wide range of futures. What is the worst that could happen? The best? Ask many **what if** questions and try to come up with stories about that possible future. What would happen if sea level rises regularly flooded your community? What if temperatures rose beyond what coffee plants can handle? What if there were major financial crises? What if Godzilla stomped on your main street? Including some scenario that will make people laugh or take notice can free up everyone's imagination—and help build comradery.

What is the range of possible futures?

Work with what is now

Many in your focus community may want to include a scenario that looks like the past. This is not realistic, given the rapid changes our world is going through. For example, the world will never go back to pre-atomic bomb days, or even pre-global pandemic days. It is important to recognize and accept the changes we have been through. But as the stockbrokers say, what worked yesterday is not guaranteed to work tomorrow!

Focus on factors

Imagining what could happen helps pinpoint weak points and leads to options to work under many futures.

There are so many factors to consider, and you can quickly get overwhelmed. However, just changing two factors can provide a wide range of stories. Climate scientists often use just temperature and precipitation to create scenarios. You can use a grid to do this. Use any two factors (flooding and funding availability, population growth and housing units) and put one factor on the vertical (x) line and one on the horizontal (y) line. Then develop a story for each area in the graph: less of both x and y, more of both x and y, more of x and less of y, and less of x and more of y.

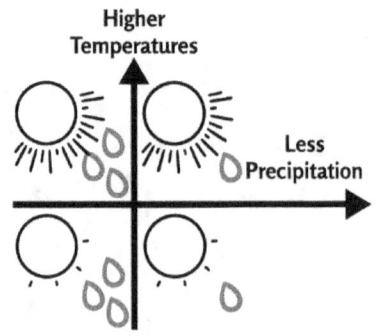

*Selfcareworldcare.wikidot.com/**scenariosworld**: how to create and consider multiple scenarios.*

What could our future look like?

Resources

What can our community use?

Inventory what you have

Knowing what you have to work with will help shape what you can do.

What do you have to work with as a community? What skills, connections, and strengths can people in your community bring to your planning? If your focus community is a neighborhood, maybe a church can provide some yard space, Oakley is a master gardner, Rowan has a lawnmower and Sally has a fence post, and nearly everyone can work to create a community garden. This is a local example of pooling resources and talents, but the idea can go much further—what resources does your community have?

Creating an inventory of the resources available to your focus community is a crucial foundation to identifying what actions are possible. Getting together as a community to brainstorm and list all of the resources affected and resources available to create options helps bring people together as their input becomes part of the change management and solution process. Poll the group and ask what we have for:

Money and time are almost always your most important resources.

- Natural ecosystem resources (such as forests, water, geographical)
- Social and economic resources (such as the economy, networks)
- People resources (such as experts, people passionate about your cause, people who can help)
- Infrastructure resources (such as buildings, roads)
- Equipment and material resources
- Time available
- Funding resources

Build from what you have

Engage people in taking inventory: What do we have? What is working now?

You can never just start from scratch—even a fire or flood that takes out your infrastructure leaves something behind to build on. Parts of the old community will remain, and you have to transform the new community using what is left from the old community and its interconnected systems (which have also changed). This is like repairing a boat while at sea—or a spaceship while out in space.

It is important to work from what does work. So look for the good! Can you expand and strengthen what is working? Once you have this inventory, examine it. Ask everyone in the community: Have we identified the resources needed to meet our objectives? If you do not have enough resources, you can figure out ways to get more resources, find other partners or help, and get creative with options.

> *I Selfcareworldcare.wikidot.com/resourcesworld: how to take inventory and bring comunty members together to share resources.*

What resources can we tap into?

What is working now?

Constraints and Limits

What can't our community do?

Roadblocks can come from limited resources, authorities like laws or traditions, physical considerations like infrastructure or ecosystems. Knowing what you do have to work with and what the boundaries actually are for your playing field is critical for developing options. Take some time to look deeper into the whys of those limits to truly understand them.

Question constraints

There are physical, legal, and other barriers to what you can and can not do.

The more mature the system is in the growth/decay cycle, the more constraints there will be and the harder it will be to get around these constraints. But these constraints may not be as rigid as they appear. However, many communities act as if once a rule or requirement is set in place, it is now set in stone forever and cannot be questioned or changed. Challenge this. Ask:

- **Are our attitudes and society rules really set in stone?** Now, no one smokes indoors. But everyone used to smoke everywhere—there are still ashtrays embedded in odd places, just like coal bins in old houses. What was unthinkable just a few decades ago is simply obvious today.

- **Is this really unchangeable?** The law is the law—until it is not. Water law in the western Unites States is a tangled, horrific, and completely unchangeable legal mess where lawsuits and fights and conflict rule the day. It can't change! But yes, actually, it can. We are nibbling at the edges of the complex beast with water marketing, water banking, flow changes, new compacts. So yes, laws can change.

The more you show solutions work, the more people will recognize what can happen and the more limits will be stretched or removed.

Work within constraints

When there are actual boundaries, explore what your focus community can do within those real limitations. Think about ways around the constraints. We can't just bulldoze over every house and rebuild so that all roofs face south for optimum solar energy. But we can put solar panels on existing roofs.

Plan for removing constraints

Identify and question the constraints in your community.

When a larger system or your focus community is shifting, then previous constraints may be completely blown away. When a hurricane or a tornado or a major wildfire destroys those same houses we said could not be optimized for solar energy, we can actually rebuild to withstand future calamities—and we can build to make the most of sun or wind power. But we have to plan for those action moments when we can address those constraints. It takes a long time to update zoning codes or to create building codes that require new safety features. But creating more flexible zoning for tiny houses or communities can help set the stage to rebuild. So plan now to act later!

*Selfcareworldcare.wikidot.com/**limitworld**: how to identify, inventory, and question constraints*

What are really constraints?

How can we break free?

How can we work within these?

Part Five:
What do we want—no matter what?

Goals/Objectives

What are our community's visions and goals?

Page: 53

Robust Objectives

What does our community absolutely need—
no matter what?

Page: 55

Aligned Objectives

Does everyone see the same vision?

Page: 57

Robust Measurements

How can we measure our impacts in the real world?

Page: 59

Goals and Objectives

Goals are overall blueprints and plans, and objectives are actions needed to get there.

What are our community's visions and goals?

Everyone in your focus community needs to understand what your community is about and what the community wants for the future. In other words, there has to be a clear direction to go in, no matter what the future brings. Once there is a dirction, a broad overall goal, then you can determine objectives (what needs to happen to get to these goals no matter what the future brings) and a strategy with actions to accomplish objectives to help your community survive and reach your goals?

Clarify your vision

Where are we going—what is the mission and vision? Our purpose and direction? When a community or country or organization sets goals, be sure they are clear to everyone in the same way. What do the goals mean and entail?

People have goals within the community, which come together as goals for the community.

Strategies with long-term goals and short-term objectives to meet those goals can work well when people widely share the same aspirations. But not asking for everyone's input up front can lead to misunderstandings and conflicts. Being mired in arguments can derail any actions that your community could take to be prepared for the uncertain futures we all face.

Strategies that everyone in your community can clearly imagine and that can provide a powerful emotional engine. Watch out for vague emotional appeals that people may interpret in very different ways, such as "Be number one again." Don't take these vague appeals at face value. Dive into what they actually mean. Being number one again in what? What is "again"? Be specific, and go back to what your community is all about!

Revisit and revise regularly

Work together to make your goals for your community clear and communicate these goals.

Remember that your strategy is not developed one time in a singe leadership retreat or workshop and we are done goal-setting for good. This is a continual process as conditions change. New people will continually come in (joining your family, moving into the neighborhood, discovering the joys of your interests, etc.) and objectives and purposes will have to be revisited again and again. This is somewhat like repairing a boat while you are at sea or fixing the starship in space as you have to refine your strategy while steering through a changing landscape.So plan these reflective actions: How will your community agree on and communicate these goals? When can your community regularly come together to revisit these long-term goals and the short-term objectives? Keep your mission and vision front and center: read it aloud at each meeting, keep it on the community website, etc.. Do whatever it takes to continue to remind your group of your common vision and the goals your focus community has set to get there.

---

*Selfcareworldcare.wikidot.com/**goalsworld**: how to create and use a community vision, strategy, goals, and objectives.*

Where are we going?
What are our goals?

Why are we here?
What is our mission?

How does everyone fit into these goals?

Robust Objectives

These are the minimal objectives would work within many futures.

What does our community absolutely need—no matter what?

When you are on a ship, the main goal is to stay afloat so that you can eventually get to port. In your focus community, sometimes the most you can do is hang on and survive. During these times, you just have to focus on the bare minimum needed to keep going. But what does that mean for your community? What is at the central core of your community? Defining your bottom line, what your community must have, helps everyone focus on ensuring that survival. For example, a small town's goals my be to increase local transportation, improve school student performance, and attract new residents. But underlying that is a robust goal: to survive as a small town and ensure that the tax base and infrastructure the town needs continues even after storms or fires.

What does your focus community absolutely need?

Robust goals define the minimum of what your community must have in whatever future comes.

Realistic goals are needed to "get down to brass tacks" or find specific goals that most in the community agree are vital to its survival (such as keeping congregations together, ensuring kids have the education they need to solve problems and thrive). Instead of grandiose and general ideals, get to the heart of your community by asking:

- Who is our community for—and who do we impact?
- Why does our community exist?
- What is the desired impact from our actions in our community?
- What are the most important things to this community?
- What can we not do without—what do we absolutely have to have to function as a community?
- What would our community need even if we were suddenly on Mars?

Work backwards from your vision

Your vision explains who your community is and what it is for. But what would be the minimum needed to embody and achieve this? What is your central, core tenet? Work backwards from your big, overarching goals.

Keep these robust goals visible

Work towards getting everyone to understand and commit to these robust, minimum goals.

These are the core ideals of your focus community. But they could be forgotten if you don't keep them—and how close your community is to achieving them in changing futures—front and center. "Out of sight, out of mind" is particularly true when you are buffeted by storms. Create reminders and continue to check back regularly as people come and go.

Selfcareworldcare.wikidot.com/robustgoalsworld: how to get to the core of your community.

What is absolutely essential for us?

What is at our core?

Aligned Objectives

Does everyone see the same vision?

When working on issues with others, it is important to develop a common mission, vision, and robust goals as a group. Otherwise, people may agree there is a problem and disagree on how to solve it—or even that there is a problem at all. Thus, working within your community to develop that sense of belonging and purpose is vital for any actions within that community. Clearly communicating the purpose and goals helps avoid conflicts and misunderstandings. George Marshall (2014) goes further as he explains that: "People will willingly shoulder a burden—even one that requires short-term sacrifice against uncertain long-term threats—provided they share a common purpose and are rewarded with a greater sense of social belonging."

Understanding everyone's perspectives and values helps build a common ground to act.

Line up objectives with others

Most opposition or conflicts occur because people feel that either their concerns were ignored or that the process is unreasonable. This stage presents many opportunities to head off these conflicts. Make sure that participants and especially potential implementors have a chance to discuss goals and understand the community's purpose and strategies. If they are not involved now, it may be very difficult to persuade them later to continue to be engaged and to work together.

Communicate to get your community working with each other rather than against each other. A community's power comes from building a collective voice.

Check in with participants

Do your objectives mesh with other existing groups? Work with these groups and bring groups together wherever possible.

Who else can get on board? Do others in your community have similar problems? What are other concerns in your community? Do they stem from the same causes as yours?

Get your message out. Use social media, create signs to raise awareness and get more people interested in these community objectives.

Keep checking in as situations change

We need to make sure that what guides us continues to show up in what we do and how we do it as our work progresses over time. We need, in other words, rituals of reflection and action to help call us and our work back into alignment with our people and purpose.

Check in with the community regularly to keep focusing on the objectives.

This is a constant avenue of communication and is vital to our communities' survival. As Erin Brockovich (2020) warns, "No one is out there working to save us; we have to start saving ourselves and creating better systems that work for all of us."

Selfcareworldcare.wikidot.com/aligngoalsworld: *how to clearly communicate, find common ground, and clarify the details in these shared goals.*

How do our actions and our goals come together?

Robust Measurements

Find measurements that will truly reflect how your indicators and vulnerable factors are doing to determine your actions' effectiveness.

More concrete actions will help paint a more realistic picture of how well your actions are working.

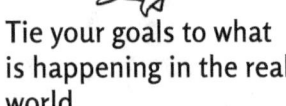

Tie your goals to what is happening in the real world.

How can we measure our impacts in the real world?

You need robust, real world measurements to judge if actions are working to meet goals and to keep your focus community's actions on track (is the situation better now? Worse? Good enough?). For example, imagine that PlasticBeGone, a local group, wants to get plastic pollution out of their river. Measuring just the number of people they talk to is not going to tell us how much trash is stil in the river. Measuring the amount of plastic in the river before and after talking to 1,000 people would be more effective to determine if talking is enough or if more measures like monthly cleanups are needed to reduce the amount of trash.

Measure what actually happens

Goals to finish a task or to have so many people at a meeting or a conference do not measure the key results: PlasticBeGone could measure the amount of plastic in the river. Or if you want to save your favorite coffee from extinction, you need to find new more sustainable methods to expand the coping range. However, your actions won't mean anything unless something happens on the ground. You can measure the number of coffee plantations saved from bankruptcy or increases in the number of shade grown coffee beans for sale. Moreover, setting a goal based on how much plastic is reduced in the world, how many coffee plantations are saved, how many women became the head of major corporations, etc. can help you focus on the how to make changes in the real world. Setting interim goals with interim actions can help. For example, create a task to remove 25 trash bags of plastic a week. This has immediate measurable results. Revisit and look at the overall picture to analyze causes and effects—and act on them. As Patrick (2019) asks: "Where is the evidence that your efforts have made a measurable result . . . in real-world data"?

How will your focus community measure achieving goals? Ask:

- How much do we want the indicators to change? Why this amount?
- How will we know when it is accomplished? Why will it matter—what changes occurred in the interconnected systems and how will those changes help your focus community?

Analyze the effects of your actions in an overall context

Of course, other factors and other actions play into these real-world measurements—not just your community's actions. Plastic choking the river could increase if everyone uses plastic disposable masks and gloves and single use bottles to combat a plague. Or could decrease if people start boycotting plastic-wrapped new products. So yes, setting these types of measurements can still be pretty fuzzy and your numbers may need to be adjusted to account for these new dynamics.

Selfcareworldcare.wikidot.com/**measureworld**: *Use indicators to set measurements, grapple with the unknowns, and tell stories about these measurements.*

What change do we want to see in our indicators?

Part Six:
What can we do?

No- and Low-Regret Options

What can we do right away?

Page: 63

Creative Options

How can everyone think outside the lines!

Page: 65

Flexible Robust Options

What actions can we use for many purposes?

Page: 67

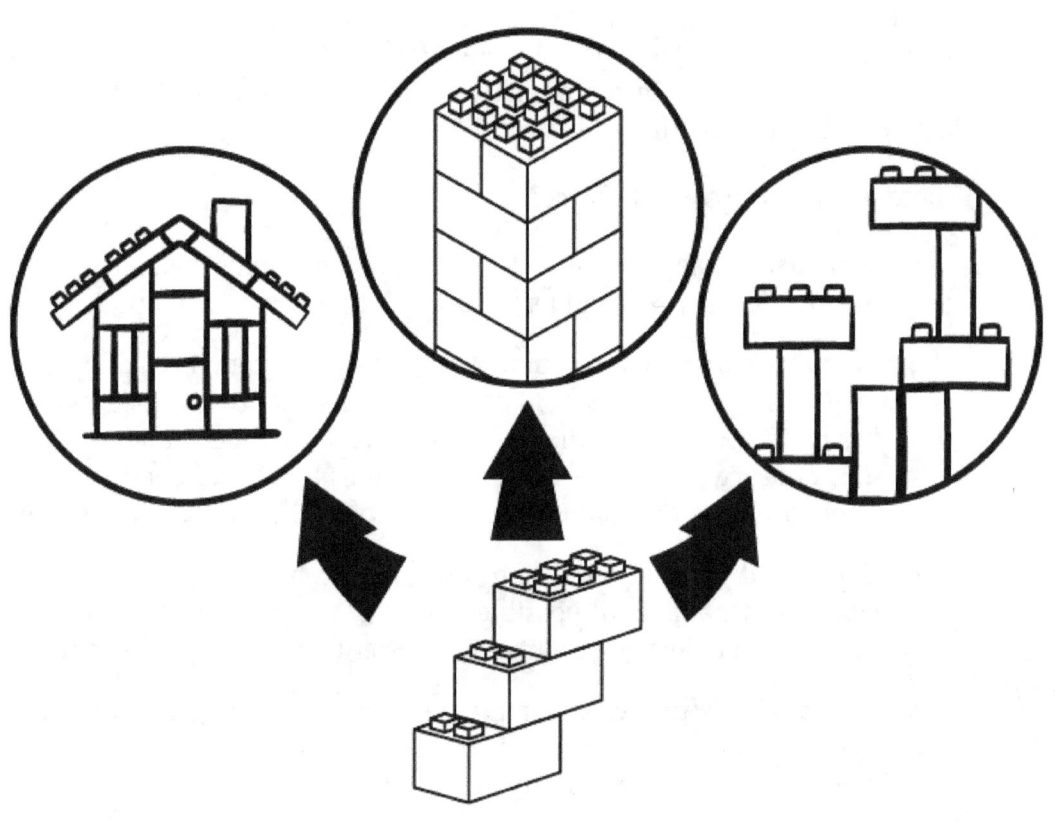

Modular Back-up Options

How can we continue if something fails?

Page: 69

No and Low Regret Options

No-regret and low regret actions are those that will help in any scenario and that you will not regret taking.

Small actions can provide big changes.

Taking actions now can help spur other actions and lay a good foundation for any future.

What can we do right away?

No-regret actions are smaller actions that can help achieve objectives, keep communities functioning, and work in a range of futures. They are cost-effective now and under a range of future scenarios and do not involve hard trade-offs. Low-regret actions are more intensive actions that we might, but probably won't regret. They are relatively low cost and provide relatively large benefits under different futures.

These no or low regret actions can be:

- **Test cases.** Using a smaller scale or a tiny test process can help pinpoint what works and lets you tinker to fine tune and optimize.

- **Stepping stones to more actions.** Planting a community garden may take some time, but it would bring your community together and create beauty in your neighborhood. Then schools could become involved in the gardens to create learning opportunities and foster good nutrition. Then local farmers could become involved, and actions can scale up.

- **Quick and short**. These can be done now to help keep your focus community going until possible futures become clearer and adaptive pathways and decision points for long-term actions become apparent.

- **Part of a long process.** Planting trees now won't help cool off hot streets tomorrow, but will be invaluable years from now. And they look nice now, so there are current and future benefits.

If even these changes prove to be too much, look for even smaller changes. These "baby steps" can be tiny nudges or little changes that can lead to larger changes much later. Instead of a full-blown community garden, perhaps start with a mint plant in a pot for each house in the neighborhood, along with notes to use mint in ice tea. This lets everyone agree on something small, gives them a taste of what could happen and thus could lead to more interest in a larger garden. Katie Patrick (2019) explains this technique and notes that "asking for a sudden big change shoots your prospect for changes in the foot. Asking for a little change puts your foot in the door."

Small changes can have a big impact. Science fiction stories are full of people who went back in time, stepped on a butterfly and changed the future. So a tiny change today can change tomorrow as well. As you start to act within your community, others can join in, and your actions become multiplied.

Moreover, in mature stages, tiny changes may be all that are possible. These actions can be as simple as talking about wicked problems like climate change with your communities and sharing concerns. Even being aware of an issue can help focus small actions to help in the long run.

> Selfcareworldcare.wikidot.com/**noregretworld**: how to avoid analysis paralysis, set up great systems, and try things out before committing to larger actions.

What small, test actions can we take now?

What can we do to prepare for emergencies?

Creative Options

Wild and crazy ideas will help find something that works to go beyond what we have always done.

How can everyone think outside the lines?

Your focus community faces wicked problems in dynamic times with lots of possible future scenarios. Whew. This is going to take more innovation and more new ideas to ensure your community can survive and thrive. So throw the gates to everyone's imagination wide open. Even the wildest ideas could lead to something that you can actually do!

- **Look into the future.** Imagine the problem is already solved—what does this future world look like when your focus communities' objectives are accomplished? What did you do? What happened?

- **Look at others.** What has worked in other communities may work for you. Some communities are planting gardens between tall buildings to provide shade below and to help clean the air. Others have created bike paths on freeways that are covered in solar panels for extra energy production as well as safer transportation.

- **Think positively.** Positive people find more solutions and can cope with adversity more effectively. Studies found that managers with greater optimism are generally better decision-makers and have more effective relationships with their staff and their bosses. When we can think positively, we can set aside group identities (us vs. them) and work together (let's address these challenges together). Patrick (2020) explains, "Fear and doom shut down your brain capacity for creative thinking. Vision and optimism superboost it."

- **Nudge.** What little thing can you do to nudge people? If you give people a convenient choice, they will take that easier route. A recycling bin close to a vending machine will encourage people to throw their cans into the recycle bin instead of the landfill. Buy what aligns with your values or talk to corporations. For example, if toys come wrapped in plastic, buy secondhand toys and tell the corporations why you did that. Vote with your money and help others do the same. As you go through your community, see what could be made just a bit more easy. Many small actions together can have bigger consequences.

- **Break hidebound rules.** How can we reach agreements to try new approaches and work around these traditional constraints and limits Some of the constraints you noted may seem completely insolvable. For example, tpeople spend their lives figuring out water law's tangled and confusing rules, and water is wasted just to keep water rights alive. We are finding innovative ways to work with the water laws to keep water in rivers and to manage flows to help fish and ecosystems, rafting, etc.? Airplane regulations cause airlines to fly nearly empty planes to keep their routes. These rules were suspended during Covid, but came back. Can we question why we need them and avoid needless emissions?

Set all minds free to dream.

Together, compete for who can come up with the craziest ideas.

*Selfcareworldcare.wikidot.com/**wildworld**: how to get everyone to come up with new and wonderful ideas.*

How many wild crazy ideas can we think of?

Make exploring the impossible possible!

Flexible Options

Make your plans flexible and adaptive to make them more robust and workable in many futures.

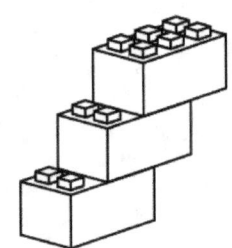

Make your plans flexible and adaptive to make them more robust and workable in many futures.

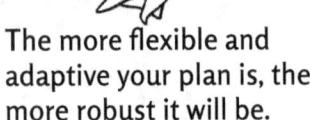

The more flexible and adaptive your plan is, the more robust it will be.

What actions can we use for many purposes?

The most effective way to plan for change is to create flexible systems that can adapt to changing circumstances. The more adaptable a system is, the more resilient it is. As you brainstorm options for your focus community, keep asking what else that idea, action, option could do. Creating one option with many purposes can save money and resources by avoiding creating multiple processes. Showing many facets of the same idea can engage different perspectives and can help get people in the community on board to adopt the idea. Your community can make a game out of this: write out each resource you identified earlier on a card. Then pick two cards and see how they could work together (like church and office building, apartment and garden).

- **How can one component serve more than one purpose?** For example, an office building could house a church on Sunday and be an emergency shelter at night. An apartment building's rooftop might make a great place for a community garden for residents. Preschools in assisted living facilities gives the adults and children more interactions. Bridges on tidal rivers could incorporate tidal turbines for power. Solar panels can cover parking lots or bikeways to provide shade and safety as well as energy. A traffic median could be planted with wildflowers for a habitat and beauty with less maintenance.

- **What in your community or in larger interconnected systems already does double duty or even more?** What systems are we working with and how can we use all of their functions? Think about a stream: fish live there, people use the water, and rafters float down the river. What type of flows can help fish, rafters, and water users?

- **How could we make actions or objects or processes more flexible during disturbances?** For example, a church building could also function as an emergency meeting place or shelter. Emergency calls could be quickly routed to either fire or police or health or a social work team—so the right people respond appropriately.

- **Use nature-based solutions.** Actively engaging nature can increase the ecosystem's flexibility—promoting natural growth and reducing the waste that will just stick around forever. For example, throwing confetti made of flowers rather than plastic during a parade can avoid polluting streets and rivers.

- **How can back up components and processes be used in more than one way?** For example, flood control along a river could be concrete spillways that are bike paths when there are no floods. Note what each resource in your resources inventory can do. What options do youu already have? What else could they do? How could this be more flexible?

Selfcareworldcare.wikidot.com/**flexoptionsworld**: *how to use multiple perspectives to find new uses for options and how to avoid rigid thinking.*

What options can be used for many purposes?

Standardized Backup Options

How can we continue if something fails?

Charity missions have built wonderful wells in villages—that no one can use now. The well worked for a while—and then a vital part failed . . . And the solution failed. There is no clean water, and girls still walk miles each day, missing out on school to get water. Ensuring that your options for your focus community can function if a particular part goes out requires both consistent parts (so you can get one to easily take its place) and backup planning. Build solutions in such a way that if one portion fails, the other portions can still function. Ask "what if. . . ?" to think through adaptive pathways.

My friend Mark, an army major, explained how the military handles uncertainty. The folks on top think they know what is going to happen—but all bets are off when the soldiers hit the ground. So the military relies on skilled people on the ground, and provides the needed resources, back up, and support to ensure that the people on the ground have the authority to adapt their tactics and handle the moment to moment decisions as they happen.

As you plan, think about addressing possible failures. Consider:

- **Backups.** If an option depends entirely on one factor, then the whole thing will crash if that single factor fails. Planning to replace a failed component can protect the process. In infrastructure, this may be a back-up power system for a water treatment plant or back-up plan to deliver water and power. In ecosystems, this may be developing separate populations of the same species. In communities, this may be people with the same training who can take over roles if someone leaves.

- **Diversification.** Put your eggs in different baskets, like investors investing in both stocks and bonds in case one of those markets fails. In infrastructure, diversification may mean ensuring there are multiple ways to handle water from floods that could compromise canals or a dam. In ecosystems, this may be a diverse range of species that occupy similar ecological niches. In communities, this may mean having different traffic routes or many food sources.

- **Failure modes.** Evaluate how each component could fail. If six out of seven roads out of the mountains would be flooded, then people will be trapped on that one road. A city that has three small water treatment plants may seem redundant. However, if there were only one large plant and that plant got clogged with ash from a fire, then the city would loseits water supply as the whole system would fail. Designing backups to backups can be important.

- **Repair plans.** Who will be there if the smallest component fails? Who will come out and change a light bulb? Where will you get that light bulb? For each component, ensure there is a workable way to fix it.

Before doing anything think through how to keep the solution functioning if there are problems.

Make it easy to swap out failing parts.

For every option you have, ask: What if this fails? And find solutions!

Selfcareworldcare.wikidot.com/backupworld: plan for the unexpected, emergencies, and setbacks.

What does this option depend on?

What if that went away?

Part Seven:
What are your strategies?

Screen for Robust Options

What options will work?

Page: 73

Evaluate Options

What workable options are the best fit?

Page: 75

Stress Test

How well does this plan work for various factors under many scenarios?

Page: 77

Timing and Scaling

How can we grow and expand community options?

Page: 79

Screen for Robust Options

Screen options to keep workable options that meet the communities' criteria and avoid fatal flaws.

What options will work?

To decide what to invest time, resources, and money in, your community must first determine which options will actually address the goals.

Fatal Flaws: Rule out options that won't work at all

What would just derail this option or cause other problems (like bringing in rabbits to eat the grass and be overrun with rabbits eating everything else, be against the law, not work well with other components or just work for a few people and not involve everyone)? Questions to flag fatal flaws include:

- Do communities want this option or at least will not actively oppose it?
- Can we do this?
- Will it meet the goals in most scenarios?

Criteria: Screen options to meet your needs

Screening every option in the same transparent way helps build understanding and trust.

Determining what options will work to achieve your goals involves setting the bar for what an option must do (your criteria) and then screening each option to only keep options that will meet those standards. Ensure options support a robust strategy that:

- Performs well over a wide range of plausible futures and keeps options open
- Trades better performance for more ability to work if our assumptions are wrong or if something unexpected happen.

Look for fatal flaws (conditions when the option just won't work). Ask:

- What are the conditions that would affect how our current or leading strategies perform?
- Under what conditions does our strategy fail to meet different stakeholders' goals?
- Is that risk possible enough that we should improve on our strategy?
- What are the cascading impacts and how would these affect your change network? (How will each action influence another action and how will each change generate another change, and yet another and so on)?
- How do we make our choices less vulnerable to uncertainties? What are the major risks and what can we do to address these risks?

Check your options to make sure they could meet the goals under a wide range of possible futures.

But don't just discard options at first glance. If there is a fatal flaw, look to see if we can adapt that option to overcome the problems.

ISelfcareworldcare.wikidot.com/robustworld: Use a screening table to compare all actions consistently

What criteria do our options need to meet?

Which workable options meet that criteria?

Evaluate Options

Seek robust plans that perform well over many futures, not optimal plans designed for a single, best-estimate future.

What workable options are the best fit?

In a community, even simple decisions get more complex—everyone has to agree on what project to tackle before they agree on how to do it! And you can not act alone: you have to work with your entire community—and beyond into the interconnected communities. Get other perspectives: What do people both in and out of your community think will work best and why? What are their values and priorities?

- **Who will do the work?** Why will they do it? How will they be paid? When will they do it? If you do not have the doers' buy in, then it won't get done.

- **Who will be affected?** Who could benefit? Who could be harmed? Think of other groups that may be affected. Family decisions affect work and schools, surfers' decisions affect fishermen, and so on.

- **What is the change network?** What else will influence the options?

Evaluate every option in the same manner. You can compare each to a no action baseline using a decision matrix. For each option, ask: *how much better would doing this be than if we did nothing at all? What are the tradeoffs and consequences?* Then you can compare those answers to see which option would be the best. Although not fixing a floodgate costs less than fixing it, damages from a flood would cost a lot more than repairs would have! Ask:

What is most important to your community and what option does the best for that?

- **How well will the plan meet our goals?** And how are we addressing the different values and priorities in the community?

- **How well will the plan work under multiple futures?** Is the plan flexible with enough backups to adapt to changes and failures? It is much more expensive to fix infrastructure later to adapt than it is to build in more flexibility from the start. Is it robust enough to bounce back from catastrophes and to work with fewer resources than are available now?

- **What are the benefits?** Options will have a varying effect—some will do more to expand the coping range or to transform the changes you want to see.

- **What are the costs and resources needed?** Options will also have a range of difficulty or cost. Some may take more time.

Work with a wide range of people to get their input. Clearly explain why and how you chose priorities.

- **Where are the weak points in any future?** What uncertainties are most important in determining the success or failure of our plans?

- **What about changes in our environment?** Will the plan still meet our objectives in a changing climate? If not, what can we do about it?

Selfcareworldcare.wikidot.com/bestworld: Calculate and evaluate regrets, measure against a no action alternative, and apply ranked criteria for a decision matrix.

What options are best for us in a range of futures?

Stress Test

Stress-testing works the plan through a range of possible actions: will they work under a wide range of possible futures?

How can you check your plan to withstand Murphy's Law (whatever can go wrong will at the worst possible time)?

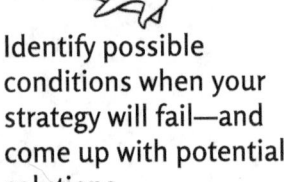

Identify possible conditions when your strategy will fail—and come up with potential solutions.

How well does this plan work for various factors under many scenarios?

Your plans depend on a lot of variables that can change in the future, and in ways you probably were not expecting. Stress-testing the plan can help pinpoint factors you depend on and strengthen weaker areas. Asking the what-ifs can help find creative ways to strengthen your plan.

What do people fear?

Asking "what if" can help bring people together as it avoids taking a stand that a particular future will happen. Moreover, it reveals what is most important to people and what they are most afraid of. This can pinpoint ways to address potential issues and help gather support. For example, if a new bus route is planned, people might oppose it as there might be more noise. Asking what if noise levels increased can help provide solutions. Perhaps a quieter motor or electric bus could be used?

What can make your plan more flexible?

If a needed component changed, would that derail your whole plan? At what point would the bus company fail if gas prices became too expensive? How can we raise that point, maybe by buying a fuel efficient bus fleet or hybrid electric buses and putting solar energy on bus parking lot roofs? What are the back-up plans if a bus breaks down?

What uncertainties are most important?

At this stage, you can ask questions about what you don't know. You have a plan that can grow and scale and adapt to many futures. You have thought about the consequences. What is still unknown? What would it take to find that information?

People may have different answers to unknown factors. So look at the plan and assume that the answer is extremely high or low. For our bus example, what would happen if the gas cost twice as much as we planned on? or five times as much? What if we had five times as many riders? Do the same thing with the answer at the other end of the spectrum (what if the costs were less or we had very few riders?). These "sensitivity analyses" change one variable and model the impacts of that change within the primary analysis. This can address uncertainty by exploring "what-if's" such as what if droughts are more severe than projected conditions indicate? What if water or power demands are higher than anticipated? What if this action performs better than modeled results indicate? When there are conflicts over data or results, these sensitivity analyses can be run and compared to the original results. These analyses can often provide more robust actions and decisions and can help build consent for actions among stakeholders, decisionmakers, and other participants.

*Selfcareworldcare.wikidot.com/**stressworld**: how to determine when plans meet and miss goals and how to test strategies. What is the difference between consent and consensus?*

What are our fears?

How can we play with our assumptions to address those fears?

Timing and Scaling

How can we grow and expand these plans?

Now that you have great options, you can plan out what to do when. Small actions (no or low regret) can grow as more people join your community. You can plan for larger actions or to expand on actions as your community grows or as needs increase and as you robustly measure these impacts.

What to do when: Examine how your plans will work over decades and centuries and from neighborhoods to nations.

Grow beyond your small community

Now you can expand your plan to grow and throughout your own focus community and other connected communities. Some ways to do this:

- **Expand your sphere of influence.** Join like-minded groups. If you are surfers who want to save the beach, talk with fishermen, etc.

- **Appeal to values and beliefs.** Think about the values that people hold and talk about how to act to uphold those values.

- **Find partners.** Who is being affected by the same changes as your community? Who has similar goals? Coordinate and come together!

Strategize for now and for later

This is where the best workable options come together for a strategy, an overall plan. Consider when and where you are going to take actions:

Start with smaller actions and plan on larger and more expensive actions as conditions change.

- **Emergency and plastic moments.** What can we prepare for? Can we imagine major changes. . . (like a storm or sea level rise that destroys infrastructure, or another pandemic that keeps everyone isolated)? How will your strategy work within futures with major changes?

- **Short term.** What actions do we need to take now? Can we take small actions and build on that success? How will we analyze our progress?

- **Long term.** Consider the long-term implications of change as you develop strategies. How will plans work within futures with long term changes, such as climate change? Solutions that address individual problems as they arise may be successful in the short term, but they may also inadvertently set into motion cascades of changes, feedback loops where changes create more changes and so forth.

- **Local.** Although climate and other major changes are happening globally, people need to react locally. What is your city and neighborhood doing to address foreseeable changes? Start at your local school or neighborhood.

- **Scale.** What actions could scale up to expand now beyond your local area and work with others locally and globally?

Think about what can happen when and how you can spread the actions.

Selfcareworldcare.wikidot.com/timingworld: how to grow in space and time and how to check in regularly to determine if more actions are needed.

How can
our plan:

grow over time?

grow with more people?

Part Eight:

Consequences and Trade-offs

How can this work for everyone?

Page: 83

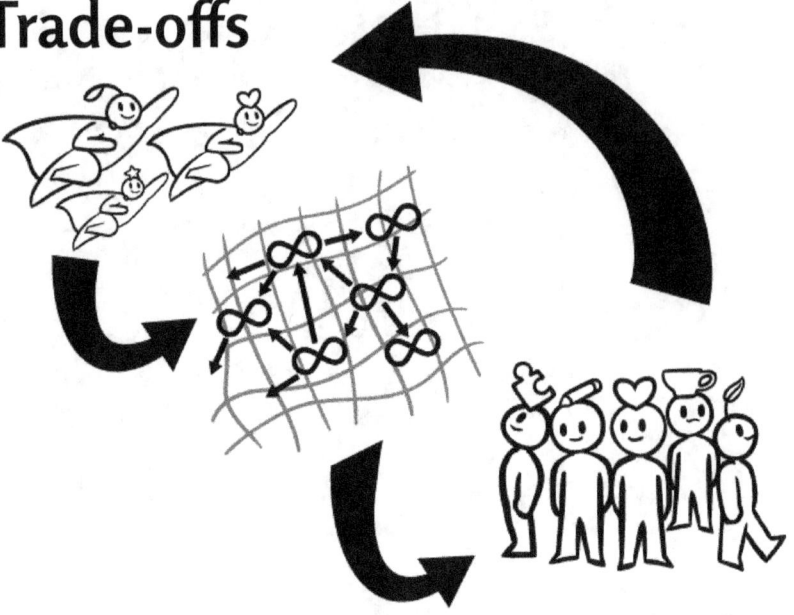

Adaptive Pathways

How can we plan for what-ifs and what-nows?

Page: 85

Implementation
Put community plans in motion!
Page: 87

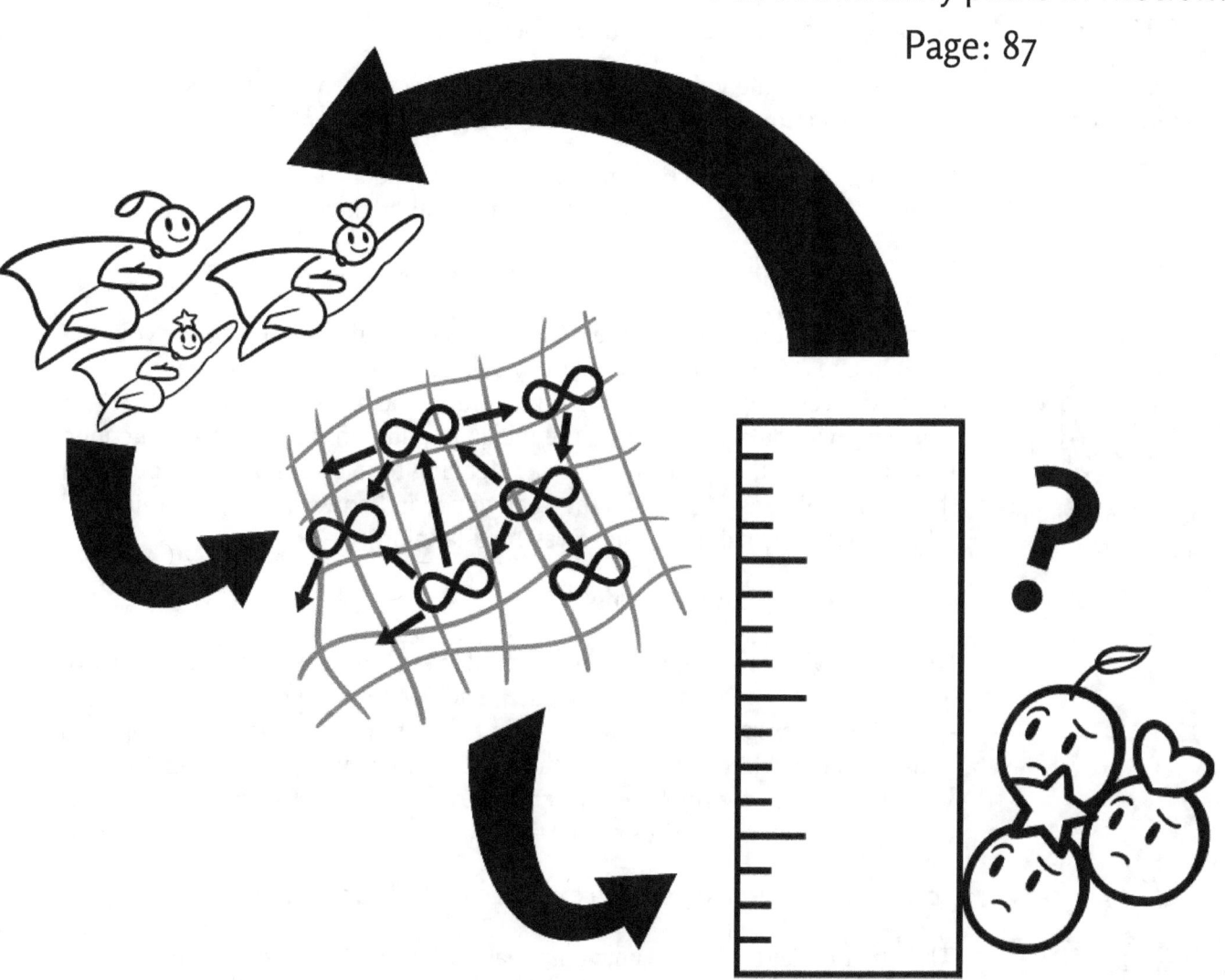

Adaptive Feedback
Keep planning and adapting!
Page: 89

Consequences and Tradeoffs

Consider all of the people, networks, and interconnected change networks and systems involved in your focus communities' actions.

How can this work for everyone?

Plans often have unintended consequences that can reverberate through your focus community and associated systems. While you can't imagine every possibility, you can identify possible issues by examining change networks:

- What else is affected by the changes you propose? How will those affected resources react? What would the secondary changes be?
- What are the risks—and who bears the burden of these risks?
- What are the vulnerabilities within this action and strategy? What will happen to our most vulnerable resources and people?

Choosing one path of action may cut off other paths. Not acting at all is a decision that may miss opportunities—and may make situations much worse.

Imagine if your plan might create other problems?

Think through the plan for potential consequences that might thwart your original aims. A famous example of this is China's war on sparrows. Sparrows were thought to eat too much grain, and so were eliminated. However, without the sparrows, the locust populations exploded and ate much more grain than the sparrows ever had, leading to mass starvation. Look at the balance already in place in the change net and how your actions might affect that (see Change Net and Systems Planning).

Who pays? Who benefits? Who is harmed?

Consider and discuss tradeoffs

No matter what the alternative, no one will ever be totally satisfied. Tradeoffs among benefits and impacts are needed, and people need to understand why the action is being taken. Focus on what true differences between the options. Is the difference large enough to matter? Is that last incremental benefit worthwhile? For example, you may have to settle for a 90-percent solution if the 100-percent solution costs four times as much.

Understand how changes affect various groups differently

Explain and explore tradeoffs with your community. What are their perspectives and concerns?

The playing field is highly uneven already. The outcomes for the changes in your community will not be the same for everyone. Examine how others, particularly vulnerable groups, will be affected—how can we protect the poor, elderly, single parents, women, people of color, etc.? These populations are hit even harder in disasters, pandemics, climate change, etc. Covid responses (shutting down public services like libraries and schools and limiting contact in nursing homes) hit etc. the hardest. Because these political and social questions were not part of the plan, there was very little in place to help these folks—even though these uneven consequences were easily predicted. So consider and consult with these groups while creating your plans and strategies.

---

*Selfcareworldcare.wikidot.com/**tradeoffworld**: how to address decisions not to act, acknowledge tradeoffs, and work with social justice.*

Where How What Who does our plan affect?

Adaptive Pathways

What to do if:
Be prepared with actions to take before a crisis or a change in conditions.

How can we plan for what-ifs and what-nows?

Since we do not know which future will come to pass, we have to plan for many possible futures. Conditions will change, and goals will shift—but having framework, a roadmap helps you act with a purpose instead of just reacting to a moment. The question is when to do something new, that is, when to change course and go from one planned pathway to another.

Plan for contingencies

Building new infrastructure is expensive and takes time, so your community needs to figure out when to start on something like that. Build the water treatment plant before you need the water. Look at your indicators: when would conditions get to a point when further actions are needed? Defining these tipping points and agreeing on resilient actions and even plans for regime shifts ahead of time will help you act quickly when the time comes.

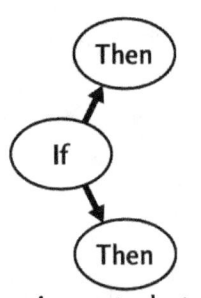

Planning out what we could do IF a scenario occurs before it happens gives us more time to adapt to that future.

Most communities are familiar with flood stage planning or other emergency plans. Emergency responders and residents are informed about what to do at each flood stage. This same "What happens if" thinking can apply to any resilience planning. Agree on what steps to take when that signpost occurs. Are there actions that stakeholders and users can agree on that could be taken at that dire point? Prepare ahead of time for actions that you could take at various sign posts. This will improve your confidence—you have a game plan now for whatever might come your way.

- What are the critical paths?
- What are the sign posts (pain/crunch/tipping points) likely to be?
- What new actions and plans can we adopt if those signposts occur?
- How can we get the resources, permits, and everything else we will need to take those actions ahead of time so we can be prepared for any action moments or plan for these regime shifts?

Plan to change course

Take time and effort to collaborate and agree on what to do if—before the if happens.

Map out these contingencies and determine who, where, how, and when your community would need to step up to the next level of action. For example, at first helping local coffee production could involve educational tours to increase local revenue and awareness about sustainable farming. These actions can continue, but might need to be augmented if temperatures rise further, causing more insect and production problems. More expensive methods like replacing varieties with more pest and temperature resistant coffee plants might be needed then. But if conditions continue to worsen, even this might not be enough, and more expensive irrigation systems may be needed.

*Selfcareworldcare.wikidot.com/**pathworld**: how to create pathway maps, identify critical paths, and plan for contingencies.*

When would we need to take new actions?

Implementation

Put community plans in motion!

Now you have a plan for what you can do in the short term (no regret actions) and when to activate a larger scale (timing and scaling) and what to do if tipping points occur (adaptive pathways). Hooray! Now do it.

Do something. Anything. But follow up by analyzing and sharing results.

Avoid analysis paralysis

You can not analyze forever. At some point, you just need to act. Even putting a tiny action in place can help people understand what can be done. So do something. Anything.

Act alone if you have to

Even if you are only one person, you can still act in your focus community. You can be a catalyst—that seed that grows a forest, the crystal that locks in every other crystal. Planting a garden or a wildflower patch in your front yard can inspire others to do the same and care for the neighborhood. One lone protestor holding up a sign can spark others to protest as well.

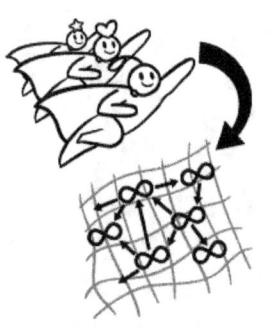

Keep communicating as you do things. Let people know what is happening where and why and what you envision the outcome will be.

Don't unilaterally act for others: Nothing for us without us

Be aware of acting for others without others. You may think this is the right thing to do, but others who are directly affected may know of other problems or factors that could be worsened. Can you meet with members of other affected communities? Reach out!

An action plan describes how each of the key study elements will be achieved so everyone can keep track of the steps and where they are going. This forms the backbone of the decision process by providing organization and direction.

Keep everyone in the loop

Acting alone and in secret is not enough. You will need to analyze your actions and publicize the results so that others can see —and do— what works. As you act, others will notice. And you will involve many more people than your focus community, as you will need experts and doers. Make sure everyone understands how you have planned, what you have considered, and how their actions fit into the larger picture. Keep your implementation plan current as you consider:

Start small and get more people and resources and actions over time.

- What resources (time, money, land, etc.) will be needed for what step?
- Who is doing what when and where?
- What actions depend on other actions or conditions?
- What can others do to partner and how can we work together?

*Selfcareworldcare.wikidot.com/**doworld**: how to publicise the costs of not acting, work with everyone, and manage projects.*

What can we do now?

Adaptive Feedback Loop

Keep measuring, analyzing, and adapting with the entire community

Keep on planning and adapting!

Yeah, you knew this was coming. It does not end here—nothing is ever won and done and finished. When you do something, measure and check and adapt. Keep examining situations and track changes. Be prepared to change course when conditions change or when the solution does not work as planned. Think of your community as a boat sailing the ocean—you have to steer with the changing currents, and you have to fix your boat while you are sailing.

Keep on checking in regularly

As your focus community, get together and discuss:

- What changes have occurred since our last decision point?
- Are our goals still appropriate? If not, what needs to change?
- Are our actions still meeting the long-term objectives?
- What do we need to tweak to ensure that the plan continues to work?

Keep on checking in and reporting to the community

Develop feedback loop by acting, getting info, adapting, and acting again. Get information and data to measure how well you are doing. Use progress bars to show how each person's effort contributes to your focus community's aligned goals. Ideally these robust measurements should as quick as possible and tailored to the individual actions, like reporting the weight of garbage going to a landfill back to a household the week the garbage can is picked up rather than delayed annual report. This helps people see the actual, real-time difference that their individual actions are making. But also report on system-wide changes as well as much as possible, so that people in and outside of your community can see these overall changes.

Keep on analyzing and adapting

The solution may not work as depicted on the drawing boards—it may need to adapt to the real world. Keep track of what has changed and why it changed.

Actions to fix complex wicked problems are experiments. We have to keep working and adapting.

- What other factors are influencing these changes?
- Can the solution work within the changed parameters?
- Can the solution address changes in needs and resources?

Going through the decision steps to address these changes will help find balanced, effective methods of dealing with the changes. Update the action plan. Include people who can support and make the changes. You might expand your scope to work with new groups and organizations.

Selfcareworldcare.wikidot.com/**loopworld**: *how to finetune forecasts, measure, and rethink.*

What worked?

What didn't?

What can we do next?

Afterwords

Planning for your community takes time and effort.

Care for your community..

Wait? What!? This is the end? I thought that this was about caring for our communities, you know, sustainable development, supporting each other, creating a caring and supportive community, maybe even a bit of business organization or project management stuff?

Yes, I can see where that could be your response to all of these planning steps and concepts for grappling with these dynamic and challenging times. And the title says "World care" which can be everything from recycling your soda bottle to inventing ways to save our planet. But to do any of that, you need to plan. And planning together helps people come together. Which is what communities are all about. When you say "this group of people all love doing this, believes this, is organized to address this, etc., you are creating something that exists beyond each person involved: you have an entity, a community. And we are all part of so many communities. Family, neighbors, interest groups, political groups, and on and on. When you can get together and discuss these questions with your community, you strengthen those ties.

Yet getting together and communicating and understanding each other's position can help everyone to work together to care for your world.

Planning in this much depth may not be for every community, and it may not be possible within the time and energy and resources available in your community. But do what you can. You now have the organizational topics and blueprint for planning:

- **Know what your community is all about.** Talk to each other. What makes you a community?

- **Analyze the situation.** What is changing? Where are the trends heading? What possible futures can you imagine? How are you affected?

- **Determine what your community needs.** Find common purposes. Where does this community want to go? What does it need to survive?

- **Brainstorm ways things you can do.** What can you put in place now that can serve you no matter what? Get a bit wild with ideas, and make sure you have back up plans.

- **Put these plans together**. Get your best options together in a plan with what to do when (timing and scaling) and what to do if (contingency planning).

- **Do it, measure it, analyze it and replan.** Keep on going through this cycle so that you can adapt to what works, what is happening, and what might happen.

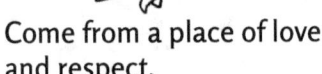

Come from a place of love and respect.

Your community will always be changing, with people entering and leaving. But you can instill these approaches to problem solving and help everyone work together, no matter what comes your way.

Selfcareworldcare.wikidot.com/references: has a list of references organized by topic, including communities and activism.

What can we do together?

References

There are many guides, many processes, many ideas. Choose what resonates for your community.

Where did those quotes come from?

As a technical writer, I am used to 50-page bibliographies. Reference materials. Back up everything with a source. And yet I tried not to do that in this paper version. I tried to simply explain conceptst that many scholars, planners, decisionmakers, project managers, etc. talk about, use, and study in many contexts. Here are the quotes I had to have.

Brockovich, Erin. 2022. Superman's Not Coming: Our national water crisis and what we the people can do about it. Penguin Random House. *This book explains the water crises facing the U.S. and the world, and explains what each of us can do about this. She gives people the tools and resources you need to be the superheros in your own communities.*

- **Introduction.** Erin Brockovich (2021) says: "Think of each and every person in your community that you can help. Remember you just need enough confidence to take that first step in the right direction."

Marshall, George. 2014. Don't Even Think About It: Why Our Brains Are Wired to Ignore Climate Change. Bloomsbury Press. *This book explains why we ignore things that threaten our communities and how we can have difficult conversations and act to address these challenges.*

Each of the concepts in this book are further explained in the website, selfcareworldcare.wikidot.com with more references to explore.

- **Aligned objectives.** George Marshall (2014) goes further as he explains that: "People will willingly shoulder a burden—even one that requires short-term sacrifice against uncertain long-term threats—provided they share a common purpose and are rewarded with a greater sense of social belonging."

Patrick, Katie. 2019. How to Save the World: How to make changing the world the greatest game we've ever played. Hello World Labs, San Francisco, California. *This book is a great step by step how to to develop robust goals that can be measured in the real world. She goes on to explain how to actually move the needle in the real world—what to measure, how to get and choose ideas to change behaviors and systems, and how to get those ideas going and people involved.*

- **Robust Measurements** . As Patrick (2019) asks: "Where is the evidence that your efforts have made a measurable result . . . in real-world data"?
- **Creative Options.** Patrick (2019) explains, "Fear and doom shut down your brain capacity for creative thinking. Vision and optimism superboost it."

Keep on reading. You and your community can do this!

These books are just a taste of the great information, analysis, and help out there.

Selfcareworldcare.wikidot.com/references: See a long list of references organized by topic, including communities and activism.

www.ingramcontent.com/pod-product-compliance
Lightning Source LLC
Chambersburg PA
CBHW082112220526
45472CB00009B/2146